WAX CRAFT.

PLATE I.

(*Frontispiece.*)

1. Encaustic wax painting from Herculaneum.

WAX CRAFT

ALL ABOUT BEESWAX

ITS HISTORY, PRODUCTION, ADULTERATION, AND COMMERCIAL VALUE

BY

T. W. COWAN, F.L.S., F.G.S., F.R.M.S., F.E.S., &c.

ISBN 978-1-4357-5078-4

TO THE

MASTER, WARDENS, AND COMMONALTY

OF THE

ART OR MYSTERY OF WAX CHANDLERS

OF THE

CITY OF LONDON

WHOSE RECORDED HISTORY OF FIVE CENTURIES

EXHIBITS ITS CARE FOR THE INTERESTS AND

DEVELOPMENT OF AN IMPORTANT INDUSTRY

ESPECIALLY AT A TIME WHEN THE CANDLES USED IN THE

RITUAL OF THE CHURCH

WERE COMPOSED ENTIRELY OF BEESWAX

THE MASTER OF THIS ANCIENT GUILD BEING

BY VIRTUE OF HIS OFFICE

PRESIDENT

OF THE

BRITISH BEE-KEEPERS' ASSOCIATION

THIS WORK IS DEDICATED

IN GRATEFUL ACKNOWLEDGMENT

BY

THE AUTHOR

PROEM.

I AM frequently asked to recommend some book treating of beeswax, but as no work on the subject has appeared for some time past, reference can only be made to text-books, which, although containing much information on bee-keeping, devote very little space to the question of beeswax.

Nearly twenty years ago I translated from the German a small pamphlet of nineteen pages on beeswax by M. J. Dennler, which found a ready sale; but this has for some time past been out of print, and, in deference to requests for a larger book, this work has been brought out, in the hope that it will supply a long-felt want for information on the subject.

Beeswax is an important article of commerce, large quantities being annually imported into this country for use in the manufacture of the finest candles, also by soap-makers and chemists in various preparations. But beyond these requirements, the extension of bee-keeping on modern methods has created a yearly demand for thousands of tons of pure wax in the production of comb-foundation for the use of bee-keepers.

From the very earliest ages, too, the manufacture of candles, figures, and flowers from beeswax was known to the ancient Egyptians, Greeks, and Romans, and I have therefore thought it well to give an historical outline of the subject, followed by separate chapters on the production of wax, its uses in commerce and manufactures.

The introduction of vegetable and mineral waxes in recent years having caused these to be used extensively for adulterating beeswax, I have treated this part of the subject at considerable length, giving detailed descriptions of these waxes, with their several characteristics, so that fraud may easily be detected.

The rendering of wax and the manufacture of comb-foundation have also been more fully dealt with than is usual in text-books.

There are districts where honey production is not profitable, owing to its being dark in colour or of an inferior quality. In such places it might be advantageous to work for the production of wax alone, the latter always being saleable.

At the end of the book will be found practical recipes for 110 various technical uses of wax, some of them containing several different recipes for choice.

With regard to the illustrations throughout the work, I am indebted to the A. I. Root Company for the use of Figs. 24, 26, and 28 to 32.

Some of the illustrations have been drawn or photographed expressly for this book, and others, alluded to in the historical chapter, have been reproduced from old engravings in my possession, which I hope will prove interesting.

This work is the result of notes and information collected during the last forty years, and I believe covers the ground more completely than any other book on the subject hitherto produced. It is hoped that it will have an equally favourable reception with that accorded to my *British Bee-keeper's Guide Book* and *The Honey-Bee.*

THOS. WM. COWAN.

Upcott House, Taunton.
June, 1908.

CONTENTS.

CHAPTER I.—HISTORICAL.

CHAPTER II.—THE PRODUCTION OF BEESWAX.

CHAPTER III.—WAX RENDERING.

CHAPTER IV.—BEESWAX IN COMMERCE.

CHAPTER V.—REFINING AND BLEACHING WAX.

CHAPTER VI.—Adulteration of Wax.

CHAPTER VII.—Manufacture of Comb-Foundation.

CHAPTER VIII.—Colouring Wax.

CHAPTER IX.—Wax Candles and Tapers.

CHAPTER X.—Manufacture of Wax Flowers, Fruits, and Figures.

CHAPTER XI.—Technical Uses of Wax.

LIST OF ILLUSTRATIONS.

WAX CRAFT.

Chapter I.

HISTORICAL.

BEESWAX was known in the most ancient times as a useful product. The Bible tells us of "a land flowing with milk and honey," and where honey was there must also have been wax. Scriptural references to honey are more numerous even than to the bee. Wax is occasionally spoken of under a distinct appellation (*donag*), differing from that of honey-comb (*nopheth*), the latter being more frequently mentioned. The natural inference is that *nopheth* was, probably, the officinal term of the period, but sacred allusions throw no light on this, being confined to comparisons and references to the fact of wax melting under the influence of heat.

When the authentic tradition of the origin of the universe was lost or obscured by the inventions of man, fable and fiction began to prevail. And to these dark ages of mythology we must turn in order to find the earliest reference to wax. We read in Greek legendary history that Dædalus, an Athenian, was the most ingenious artist of his age. He is credited with many inventions, not the least being the use of sails for ships. Having killed his nephew Dalus, he fled with his son Icarus from Athens to Crete. Here they made for themselves wings of feathers and wax, and took their flight from Crete. According to the legend, Icarus attempted so high a flight that, nearing the sun, the wax cementing the wings to his body was melted, and, falling into the Ægean Sea, he was drowned near the island called after his name. The father, flying at a lower elevation, alighted at Cumæ, in Italy, where he built a temple to Apollo. (*See* Figs. 2 and 3, Plate II.)

Then we read in the Second Eclogue of Virgil that the god "Pan taught to join with wax unequal reeds"—this in allusion to his invention of a musical instrument composed of seven reeds. Pan was also supposed to have been the guardian of bees.

Pausanias tells us that one of the oldest

2

3

2. Dædalus fixing the wings with wax on his son Icarus

3. The descent of Icarus into the Ægean Sea

4

5

4. Roman maidens with tablets of wax

5 Open tablet and style

temples dedicated to Apollo was raised by bees from wax and wings, and was sent by the latter to the Hyperboreans.

The Greeks, Phœnicians, and Romans were acquainted with beeswax, and even understood how to bleach it. Pliny calls white wax *cera punica* (Punic wax), and refers to its preparation and bleaching in the following words:—"The best wax is known as Punic, or Carthaginian wax, the next best being a wax remarkably yellow in colour and permeated with the smell of honey. This last comes from Pontus, and it is surprising to find it in no way affected by the poisonous honey it has contained. The next in quality is Cretan wax, which contains the largest proportion of propolis, a substance of which we have previously made mention when treating of bees. Next to these varieties comes Corsican wax, which, being the produce of the box-tree, is generally thought to be possessed of certain medical properties.

"The Punic wax is prepared in the following manner:—Yellow wax is first blanched in the open air, after which it is boiled in water from the open sea, with the addition of some nitre. The flower of the wax—or, in other words, the whitest part of it—is skimmed off with spoons, and poured into a vessel containing a little cold water. It is then again boiled in sea-water by itself; this done, the vessel is left to cool. This operation is three times repeated, and the wax is then left in the open air, exposed upon a mat of rushes, to dry in the light of the sun and moon respectively, for while the latter adds to its whiteness, the sun helps to dry it. In order, however, that the wax may not melt, it is covered with a linen cloth; thus refined, if it is boiled once more, the result is a wax of the purest whiteness. Punic wax is also considered the best for medicinal preparations."

In the first century of our era—during the time of Dioscorides, a physician and botanist of Greece—wax was rolled into sheets for making artificial flowers according to a method described by him.

In ancient Greece and Italy bee-keeping was of great importance to the farmer, the proceeds of wax and honey forming a valuable part of his revenue. Even the poorest peasant kept bees, not only for the honey but also for the wax, as being equally valuable.

The ancients down to the Middle Ages used wooden tablets covered with a thin layer of wax, on which they traced the characters with a metal style, pointed at one end and flattened at the other. They were used for correspondence and for temporary inscriptions, but when permanency was required it was usual to engrave the inscription on marble, brass, or leaden sheets. Paper only came into use about the thirteenth century.

After alluding to the leaves of the palm and the bark of trees as being used for writing on, Pliny says:—"In succeeding ages public documents were inscribed on sheets of lead, while private memoranda were impressed upon linen cloths, or else engraved on tablets of wax. Indeed, we find it stated by Homer that these tablets were employed for this purpose even before the time of the Trojan war."

The tablets referred to were in the form of a book (Figs. 4 and 5, Plate III.), the respective boards having a raised border round them, so that when closed the wax surfaces were preserved from friction for the protection of the writing. When folded, they were sealed with wax and impressed with a device engraved usually on a ring worn by the writer. When the writing was no longer needed, the waxen surface was smoothed down with the flat end of the style.

These tablets consisted of two, three, or more leaves, and according to their number they were called: *diptycha*, with two; *triptycha*, with three; *penteptycha*, with five leaves; and those that had more were called *polyptycha.* Catullus tells us that the ancient Romans generally wrote their love-letters on these tablets, and that the person receiving them replied on the same, after smoothing out the first writing. These tablets are illustrated in Figs. 4 and 5, Plate III.

In the fourth century, during the annual ceremony of the Paschal candle, a large wax candle was blessed and placed on the altar on the day before Easter. At that time the candle used was not intended to be burnt at all, for it had no wick, being simply a column of wax upon which all the movable feasts of the year were inscribed.

It was quite natural that such a malleable and plastic substance as wax should be utilised in the fine arts of the period; we therefore find it used by painters and sculptors of the time in considerable quantities. Waxen profiles seem to have been the favourite likeness with the Romans for such magistrates as had the right to sit in the curule chair. Pliny tells us also that "portraits modelled in wax were arranged, each in its separate niche, to be always in readiness to accompany the funeral processions of the family—occasions on which every member of the family that had ever existed was always present."

When a man became celebrated, his figure, in wax, appeared in the atrium of the private house, as well as in public buildings.

Masks, taken after death and used in funeral processions, were ultimately cast in wax (Fig. 11, Plate VI.). According to Pliny, "the first person who expressed the human features by fitting a mould of plaster upon the face, and improving it by pouring molten wax into the cast, was Lysistratus of Sicyon, brother of Lysippus. It was he, in fact, who made it his study to secure a faithful likeness of the person represented. Before his time the only thought of the artists was how to make their portraits as handsome as possible."

Wax figures of their deities were used in the funeral rites of the ancient Egyptians, and deposited among other offerings in their graves. Among the early Greeks wax figures were used as dolls for children.

Modelling in wax was also common in the earlier centuries of our era, the Emperor Valentinian being recorded as highly accomplished in the art, which during the sixteenth and seventeenth centuries attained a high standard of perfection. Copying the Italians, both German and Spanish artists produced numbers of portrait medallions, busts, and statuettes, as well as groups clothed with gorgeous garments, which portraits were generally admired for their fine execution.

During the reign of Louis XIV. Antoine Benoist, a celebrated artist, was designated as "painter to the king and sole sculptor in wax." A wonderfully fine portrait, executed in beautifully coloured wax by this artist, is still preserved at Versailles. He was granted a patent of nobility by Louis XIV., and his coat of arms consisted of three sable bees on a gold ground. Benoist's fame also spread abroad, and he made busts in wax of the courtiers of Anne of Austria, which he was allowed to exhibit in Paris. He was also invited over to England, where, amongst other portraits in wax modelled by him, was one of James II. and the attendants of his Court.

Benoist made a fortune from his skill in wax portraits, but soon had imitators. It became the fashion during the funeral ceremonies of princes and persons of distinction to exhibit their effigies modelled in wax, and there are numerous records of this prevailing custom, ranging from the time of Philip of Valois in 1350 to the Prince of Condé in 1646, after which date there seems to be no further record.

The latest and most perfect figures modelled

in wax are to be seen at Madame Tussaud's in London, the Grevin Museum in Paris, along with those seen in the windows of hairdressers and in travelling shows of wax-works.

In Italy all the early bronzes were cast from models in wax, and about the end of the eighteenth century the sculptor Flaxman made a number of portraits and other figures in wax.

Painting in wax seems to have been practised many centuries ago, for Anacreon, addressing an artist who was painting the Bacchantes, makes allusion to the wax used for the purpose, showing that its solubility in oils and fats was known even in those days. Pliny tells us that in his time it was not agreed who was the original inventor of the art of painting in wax and in encaustic, some thinking that the credit of the discovery should be given to Aristides of Thebes, who was the first of all painters to give full expression to the mind and passions of man, although he was somewhat harsh in his colours. Subsequently, however, the art was brought to perfection by Praxiteles.

This method of painting was practised to a great extent from the time of Alexander the Great until the seventh or eighth century, from which time it gradually declined until the fourteenth century, when it seems to have fallen into disuse, and all practical knowledge of the art became entirely lost. Long afterwards—about 1750—interest in the forgotten art was recovered, and the practice of it revived in France by M. Bachelier and Count Caylus. It was also restored in Munich in the reign of King Louis of Bavaria. Since that time many fine works in this style of painting have been produced. The colours are ground and laid on with a vehicle composed principally of wax. This is brought to the surface either by the application of a warm iron, such as is used in laundry work, or by a vessel containing fire being held a little distance from the picture.

Referring to painting with minium, Pliny tells us that the proper way is to first "dry the wall, then with a hair-brush apply hot Punic wax, melted with oil, after which the varnish must be heated with an application of gall-nuts burnt to a red heat till it quite perspires. This done, it must be smoothed down with rollers made of wax, and then polished with linen cloths till it shines like polished marble."

Pliny also says that in ancient times only two methods of encaustic painting were in use, viz., in wax and on ivory, with the cestrum or pointed graver, but we learn that when this art was extended to the painting of ships of war a third method was adopted, that of melting the wax colours and laying them on with a brush while hot. Such painting applied to ships was said never to spoil from the action of the sun, salt water, or winds. It is certain that this method of painting resisted injury caused by time and the elements, for the vast mural paintings taken from patrician houses in Herculaneum and Pompeii, that can still be seen after the lapse of more than eighteen centuries, bear witness to the wonderful preservation of these colours. The frontispiece (Plate I.) is a good example of one of these paintings.

Witchcraft and sorcery are nearly as old as the world, so that it is not surprising to learn that a substance almost imperishable like bees-wax should be employed by sorcerers and witches, whose spells were frequently resorted to with criminal intentions.

When the magician or witch desired to cast a spell on anyone, an image of wax representing the victim was made, and surrounded with three (the fatidical number) different coloured threads, each thread having three knots. The image was then pierced with needles in a number of places, sometimes all over, and exposed in the streets of Athens, and the individual on whom the spell was cast was supposed to experience similar

tortures in the same parts of the body as the effigy would feel if alive. Sometimes this was done in order to obtain a favour, but more often vengeance was the object of these cabalistic proceedings, and if the victim did not succumb to fright, poison was used by the sorcerer to obtain the desired end.

In all these sorceries and bewitchings it was considered of great importance that the features of the person aimed at should be copied as accurately as possible in wax. If the needles already mentioned penetrated the heart or head of the figure, the bewitched person was supposed to die, and no doubt sometimes did from sheer fright or superstition.

In the history of the early Egyptians we also find that charms and miniature wax figures were used for divers purposes by magicians of the period. From a papyrus of the time of the Third Rameses we learn that a certain conspirator had modelled for himself waxen figures of men and had them enchanted with mystic words for the purpose of winning the favour of the women of this Pharaoh's harem.

Grecian magicians also made use of wax figures and honey, pretending to foretell events and predict death by their means, and fatal results sometimes occurred through fright and belief in the magician's powers. The Romans, too, evidently used such figures, for we find that Ovid, in one of his elegies, complains of being under the malicious influence of a statue made of red wax which bore his image and name. Then, centuries later, the French historian Mezerai refers to the malicious incantation of Charles of Valois, as revealed in a document dated 1564, which states that the effigy of wax "was made, having the resemblance of the king lying on a bed of sickness, and had this not been discovered, it was intended to make the king die of a lingering death by placing the wax image near the fire, and as the effigy gradually melted away the life of the king (as they supposed) would also fade away, until death supervened."

In the chapter in his "Laws" relating to poisoning and sorcery, Plato says:—"And when men are disturbed in their minds at the sight of waxen images, fixed either at their doors, or in a place where three ways meet, or on the sepulchres of parents, there is no use in trying to persuade them that they should despise all such things because they have no certain knowledge about them." He then goes on to explain what is to be done with those given to poisoning or witchcraft, and concludes by saying:—"But he allowed themselves this luxury (as it was then held to be) were accounted extravagant.

One of the first examples of public lighting dates back to the beginning of the fourth century, when the Emperor Constantine ordered the whole city of Constantinople to be illuminated on Christmas Eve by means of lamps and wax candles.

From the very earliest times candles were associated with religious ceremonies. According to the established rites of Zoroaster, the pagans burned lighted candles in their worship of the Sun-god. What was done on a grand scale on certain high occasions in connection with this sun-worship was repeated on a smaller scale in the individual acts of worship to their several gods by lighting lamps and wax tapers before their favourite divinity. In pagan Rome the same practice prevailed, and in their processions wax candles figured largely. They were also used in the celebration of the Eleusinian mysteries, held in Attica in honour of Ceres, the goddess of corn, and in remembrance of her favours. That there was some occult "mystery" connected with the use of wax candles may be readily believed if we bear in mind the unanimity with which different pagan peoples have agreed to use them in their sacred rites. In the worship of Ceylon wax candles are considered an indispensable requisite, and devotees are obliged to place them before the image of Buddha.

At all the principal festivals of Saturn, Bacchus, and Ceres, candles and wreaths made of wax were much used.

From a papyrus of Rameses III. we gather that payments were made from the royal treasury of sacrificial funds, such as the following:—

331,702 jars of incense, honey, and oil.
3,100 teben of wax.
1,933,766 jars of incense, honey, fat, oil, &c.

The early Christians, who at one time met only in the catacombs, made use of this method of lighting, and afterwards, when permitted to build churches, they found the sacred edifices so dark as to compel the use of candles for the purpose of illumination. It was not until the fourth century that lights began to be employed for ritual and symbolical purposes, while at a later period the Roman and Eastern Churches commenced using them in the daytime, and from this time onward the consumption of wax for this purpose gradually increased.

At funerals also, from the days of Constantine, processional lights were used, and it was a common practice to have lighted candles placed round a corpse before interment or cremation.

In the city of Fez, on Mahomet's birthday, the scholars of every school celebrated a feast, every boy carrying a lighted torch, some of which weighed 30 lb. Purchas tells us that these torches were most curiously made, "being adorned round about with divers fruites of Waxe, which being lighted betimes in the morning doe burne till Sun rising, when the solemnity ceaseth. This day useth to be very gainful unto the School-masters, for they sell the remnant of the Waxe upon the Torches for above a hundred Duckets."

It was formerly a custom of the priests to distribute the remains of the Paschal candle among the people, who burnt it in their houses and on their lands as a preservative from harm. From this custom originated also the *Agnus Dei,* a cake of wax stamped with the figure of a lamb with a nimbus, bearing a cross or flag. Such medallions are still used in the Church of Rome and are blessed by the Pope at intervals, beginning with the first Sunday after Easter following his consecration, and every subsequent seventh year.

In his "Encyclopædia of Antiquities" T. D. Fosbrook tells us that during the Middle Ages candles were not made by regular craftsmen, but by monks and the servants of the nobility. An illustration of this is to be found in Asser's "Annals," where an account is given of the manner in which King Alfred directed his candles to be formed. "He commanded his chaplain to supply wax in sufficient quantity, and he caused it to be weighed in such a manner that when there was so much of it as would equal the weight of seventy-two pence, he caused the chaplain to make six candles thereof, each of equal length, so that each candle might have twelve divisions marked across it." These candles, when burnt in succession, lasted for twenty-four hours, and each division indicated the third of an hour.

The Reformation severely affected the wax trade, and bee-keeping also suffered heavily in consequence, from the fact that the Evangelical Church did away with the use of tapers at Divine service.

In addition to tapers and candles, wax was used in still larger quantities in the manufacture of artificial flowers and fruits, which were much used as ornaments for rooms, artificial flowers made of woven fabrics being then unknown.

The making of fruits and flowers in wax was brought to great perfection in Rome and also in Alexandria. Varro praises the skill of the Roman wax-worker Posis, who made apples and bunches of grapes so like Nature that it was impossible to distinguish any difference at sight between the real and the artificial.

Lampridius, the historian, mentions that Heliogabalus had served for the guests at his table imitations in wax of all the food partaken of by himself.

In very ancient times wax was occasionally used to fashion the miniature figures of ancestors, kept in houses to be produced on certain important ceremonial occasions. It was also used for making images of animals for people too poor to buy living animals for sacrificial purposes.

Besides these curious customs, it is recorded that at the Adonis festival waxen figures of fruit and animals were placed by women about the catafalque, upon which was an image of the god, and at the same time little figures of the god were brought out to public view.

In pagan times votive offerings in wax were very plentiful in the temples, and such of them as took the shape of figures came into use in the Roman Catholic Church; indeed, so numerous were they in Italy that the walls of the Church of the Annunciation in Florence were completely covered with them. From the Middle Ages onward it was the custom to burn candles before a Madonna or saint whose favour was sought.

Devout people at that time firmly believed that their wishes would be granted through the influence of wax images, and adopted this form of giving thanks for expected blessings to come. In Germany and other countries the shape of that portion of the body of persons affected by disease was moulded in wax and placed in the church with the conviction that in this way recovery would be ensured. Even to this day one may sometimes see in chapels and on the altars in places of pilgrimage hands, feet, arms, and other parts of the body formed in miniature from wax.

In making candles intended to be placed on the altar during Mass only pure wax was employed, those made of tallow or other substances being used only for the purposes of illumination.

For medical purposes certain valuable properties of wax have been recognised from the earliest ages, Greek and Roman chemists attributing hypothetical virtues to this substance, and profiting by it at the expense of their credulous patients. Pliny tells us that "every kind of wax is emollient and warming, and tends to the formation of new flesh; fresh wax is, however, the best. It is given in broth to persons troubled with dysentery, and the combs themselves are sometimes used in a pottage made of parched alica. Wax also counteracts the bad effects of milk, and ten pills, the size of a grain of millet, will prevent milk from coagulating in the stomach."

Some idea of the extent to which wax was used in commerce in distant ages may be gathered from what Pliny further says:—"As to the different uses to which wax is applied in combination with other substances in medicine, we could no more make an enumeration of them than we could of all the other ingredients which form part of our medical compositions. These preparations, as we have already observed, are the result of human invention. Cerates, poultices, plasters, eye-salves, antidotes—none of these have been formed by Nature, that parent and divine framer of the universe; they are merely the inventions of the laboratory, or rather, to say the truth, of human avarice." He also tells us that the juice of the laser-wort mixed with wax will extract corns from the feet after they have been first loosened with a knife, and as a remedy for convulsions it is given in pills (coated with wax) about as large as a chick-pea.

Wax was also employed for a great number of other purposes. Urns and other vessels used for holding wine, oil, and metheglin were sealed with it. Mixed with such other ingredients as brick-dust, lime, or pitch, it formed a cement for internal architectural decorations. In a pure condition ropes were smeared with it in order to preserve them from rotting, and the colours of walls and marbles were improved by being polished with this substance.

Regarding embalming the dead, Herodotus tells us " the Persians cover the body with wax and then place it in the ground." Strabo also says their mode of burial was to smear the bodies over with wax before interment. The Assyrians also, who had many rites in common with the Persians, placed their dead in honey after smearing the body with wax. The Egyptians likewise did this at times, although it was not a usual custom with them.

The Romans first used wax for seals of deeds and legal documents, but for this purpose it was generally mixed with some other ingredient that would tend to harden the wax, in addition to the various colours incorporated with it. The mixture varied at different epochs, and the colours were also changed according to the dignity of the persons and the nature of the deeds to which they were affixed. Specially fine seals were usually covered with circular pieces of paper to ensure their preservation.

Shakespeare alludes to the use of wax in sealing documents in the "Second Part of King Henry VI.," where the rebels under Jack Cade met at Blackheath. On this occasion one of the rebellious crowd says:—"The first thing we do, let's kill all the lawyers." To which Cade replies:—"Nay, that I mean to do. Is not this a lamentable thing, that of the skin of an innocent lamb should be made parchment? that parchment, being scribbled o'er, should undo a man? Some say the bee stings: but I say, 'tis the bee's wax; for I did but seal once to a thing, and I was never mine own man since." Shakespeare makes several other references to wax being used for this purpose.

After all that has been said, one is apt to wonder how the enormous demand for wax could have been supplied in the ages long past to which reference has been made. It becomes clear, however, that it was usual to impose taxes which had to be paid in certain quantities of wax. In the year 181 B.C. Prætor

Pinarius, after defeating the inhabitants of the island of Corsica, imposed on them a tax of 100,000 lb. of wax, and this contribution was doubled two years afterwards. The inhabitants of Trebizond also paid tribute to the Romans in equivalents of wax. In the Middle Ages taxes in the form of wax were paid to kings, and certain officers had the right to demand a given number of candles and pounds of wax.

In all religious ceremonies in France large quantities of wax were consumed, and the incumbents neglected no means of procuring it. Among the annual revenues of the Bishop of Puy was 20 lb. of wax. In 1330 the farmers of the domain of Beauregard had each to pay 2 lb. of wax annually. In 1632 John de Frettar, sexton of the monastery of Chaise Dieu, stipulated for an annual rent of 600 lb. of wax, to be of good merchantable quality, that the tenant was to bring to his house yearly on St. John's Day. Another deed, dated July 27, 1668, shows that the monks of the same monastery rented to John Marel for six years the revenues of the workroom for the payment of 120 lb., to be paid in wax candles of first quality at the rate of 18 sols per lb.

The employment of candles, which up to

that time was chiefly confined to churches, monasteries, and houses of the nobility became very general in the fifteenth century, and the trade of candle-making had acquired so much importance that the wax chandlers of London obtained an act of incorporation. This Guild (one of the oldest) is now known as the Worshipful Company of Wax Chandlers.

There is no documentary evidence of this ancient Company's existence prior to 1371, but from a petition presented to the Court of Aldermen in that year it would appear the Guild had then attained an established position.

In 1483 (1 Richard III.) the Company was incorporated by Royal Charter, with power to choose a Master and two Wardens to oversee the craft of wax chandlery, and, upon any defects or defaults being found, to punish the offenders. This charter was confirmed and extended by subsequent charters.

Grants of arms were conferred in 1485 by Sir Thomas Holme, Clarenceux King-of-Arms, and in 1536 the arms were altered and amplified by Thomas Hawley, Clarenceux King-of-Arms, and again in 1636 were confirmed by Henry St. George, Richmond Herald.

By-laws based upon the charters were confirmed in 1515, and again in 1664.

PLATE IV.

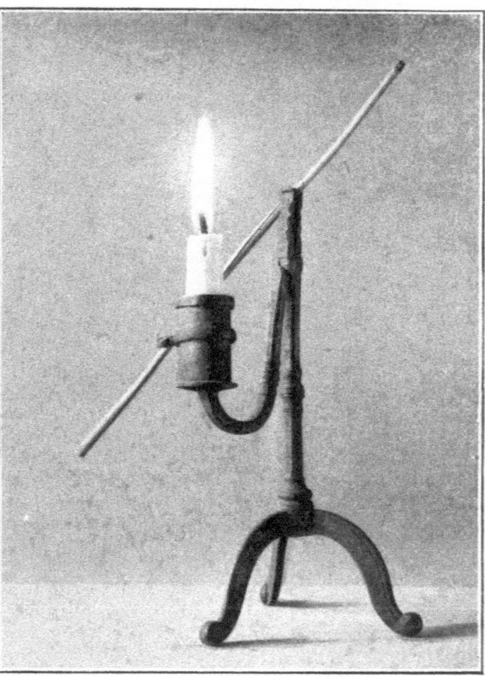

6 7 8

6. Normansell cup 7 Rushlight holder with candle. 8 Beadle's staff-head.

PLATE V.

9

10

9 and 10. Engraved designs on Normansell cup

The Company's books contain many references to faulty wax and the punishment of offenders, the punishment generally being the forfeiture of the wax, wrought or unwrought. Links, staff torches, &c., unprinted, " corse cast," and badly made links, and mixing wax with adulterants seem to have been the principal offences.

The Company had, in common with its sister Companies, parted with its most valuable plate, which, according to a seventeenth-century record, must have been an exceedingly fine one. Among the pieces that remain, the most interesting are the Normansell Cup, of classic design (Figs. 6, 9, and 10, Plates IV. and V.), and the Beadle's Staff-head (Fig. 8, Plate IV.).

The following description of the cup, sent by the Wax Chandlers' Company, appears in the catalogue of antiquities and works of art exhibited in May, 1861, at Ironmongers' Hall:—
"A large straight loving cup and cover (silver), 20½ in. high, 6¾ in. diameter, on a baluster stem and a round foot; on the cover stands a gilt figure of Mars, with a spear and shield, all of very rough execution. The cup is engraved over the whole surface with subjects and articles relating to the production and manufacture of wax. On the bowl is a man tingling a

swarm of bees, and another is hiving the same from the bough of a tree; and two shields of arms, viz.: 1st, the arms of the Company; 2nd, argent on a fess cotised azure three fleurs-de-lis, or, for Normansell. Crest, a demi-female holding in her left hand an annulet, and inscribed:—'The Gift of Richd. Normansell, Gent., Tenant to ye Companie.' On the cover are the following subjects:—On a table stands a taper-roller fitted with scissor-snuffers; a melting cauldron on a fire, a man with ladle in front of a fireplace, accompanied by his turnspit; a naked figure kneeling at a desk, at the side of which is a large taper, which he appears to have just lighted; a robed female with basket on her head, and with a sickle cutting cotton for the wicks from a tree; on the foot are figures in Eastern costumes, bee-hives on stands, a griffin on a pedestal, birds, &c. The plate mark is the small black letter **f**, of 1563."

The Beadle's Staff-head, probably made about 1670 or 1680, is thus described in the *City Press* of March 13, 1897:—"It is of somewhat irregular shape, and is covered with a design in high relief incorporating the Company's arms and motto. Below this is a representation of a bee-hive and bees, illustrating the trade of wax-making."

It will therefore be seen that formerly bee-keeping must have been carried on extensively, as honey was the only sweetening substance, but by the introduction of sugar bee-keeping was decreased and the production of wax was reduced to a minimum. Besides the Reformation, which reduced the demand for wax, powerful competitors appeared in commerce, and wax obtained from various plants and minerals, such as stearine, paraffin, ceresin, and others, which are frequently used for the purpose of adulterating beeswax, further lowered its price.

At the present time the Greek Orthodox Church makes the largest use of wax, for this and oil are the only illuminating agents allowed. In the Roman Catholic Church the "Catholic Dictionary" says:—"The present custom of the Church requires that candles should be lighted on the altar from the beginning to the end of Mass, nor can lighted candles be dispensed with on any consideration. A parish priest, for instance, must not say Mass for his flock, even on a Sunday, unless candles can be procured." These, as well as candles for weddings, fêtes, and saints' days, are generally ornamented either with spirals of gold or with different devices in colours. The small candles used on Christmas-trees are also made of coloured wax. Besides candles, wax is also used for making thin tapers, and for a number of artistic, medicinal, and technical purposes.

The modelling of anatomical dissections, first practised in Florence, is now common, and many fine specimens can be seen in museums.

Chapter II.

THE PRODUCTION OF BEESWAX.

BEESWAX has its origin in the honey consumed by bees and transformed by them into fatty matter by a process of digestion and secretion.

This, however, was not the opinion of ancient writers—Swammerdam, Maraldi, Réaumur, and others, who, being aware of the fact that numerous plants were capable of producing wax-secretions, for a long time held the opinion that bees collected ready-made wax directly from flowers, and, when building their comb from it, merely had to knead the wax so gathered with saliva in order to render the substance more pliable for working with.

Wax exists as a vegetable product, and forms a part of the green fecula of many plants, particularly of the cabbage. It may also be extracted from the pollen of most flowers and from the skins of plums, among other stone fruits. It also constitutes a varnish upon the surface of the leaves of many trees, while the berries of *Myrica angustifolia*, *latifolia*, and *cerifera* afford abundance of wax. But this so-called vegetable wax, when chemically examined, is found to be either not wax at all, but only ordinary fat, i.e., a compound including glycerine, or simply a waxy matter somewhat allied in composition to beeswax, but materially differing from the latter in other respects.

We now know that beeswax is not found ready made in Nature, but is formed in the body of the worker-bee. It is an organic and not a mechanical production, and issues in the form of scales from between the ventral plates of the abdomen.

It is difficult to say who was the first to notice these wax-scales, but Martin John in 1684 mentions them, as did Thorley in 1744 and Wildman in 1779. Hermann C. Hornbostel, a Hanoverian pastor, also describes them in the "Hamburg Library" about 1745. On August 22, 1768, M. Willelmi, writing to M. C. Bonnet, said that a German peasant, member of a society of bee-keepers, had ascertained that wax was produced in the shape of scales between certain of the rings on the under side of the abdomen (Fig. 16, Plate VIII.). Unfortunately, M. Willelmi does not mention the name of this Lusatian peasant, but states that the wax-scales can be removed with the point of a needle from a bee working at comb-building. Subsequently John Hunter in 1792 gave a description of the segments of the bee's abdomen, and drew attention to the wax-glands by which these scales were produced. F. Huber in 1793 commenced a series of experiments, which eventually confirmed the discovery, showing that wax was produced from honey, and not gathered, as was supposed by Réaumur and others.

On each of the four ventral plates in the body of a worker-bee is a framework of chitine surrounding two transparent surfaces. One of these ventral plates is seen enlarged in Fig. 17, Plate VIII., showing the transparent surfaces on which the wax-scales are produced. The dark part marks the hard chitine framework surrounding the discs, while the transparent wax-yielding surfaces are irregular, pentagonal in shape, and covered by the segment immediately above them. The lower part, which overlaps the plate below it, is of hard chitine and covered with feathered hairs. The smooth, slightly sunken surfaces are the moulds in which are formed the wax-scales from the secretion which passes through them in a liquid state from glands situated beneath. These wax-secreting glands are only found immediately under the transparent membrane, and do not exist beyond the framework. The fat-cells are connected with the membrane by tubes, through which the liquid wax flows upwards, and passes through the membrane when the temperature is at 95 deg. to 98 deg. Fahr.

The fluid wax is thus moulded on the depressed cavities; the hard part of the segment above, pressing over them, causes the liquid to assume their shape, and the little scales, after becoming solid, are drawn out of these so-called wax-pockets as required for use.

Wax cannot be produced at all times, but its secretion is voluntary, and for its production a temperature of from 87 deg. to 98 deg. Fahr. is required, which the bees are able to obtain by close clustering when comb-building (Fig. 14, Plate VII.). The wax-scales resemble mica, are transparent, very brittle, pale yellow in colour, and at such times they protrude from beneath the segments, as seen in Fig. 16, Plate VIII. These wax-scales may be found in abundance scattered on the floor-board of a strong colony during the time when the bees are busy comb-building. They are removed from the cavities by means of the pincers on the hind legs, transferred to the front legs, and then to the mouth,

PLATE VI.

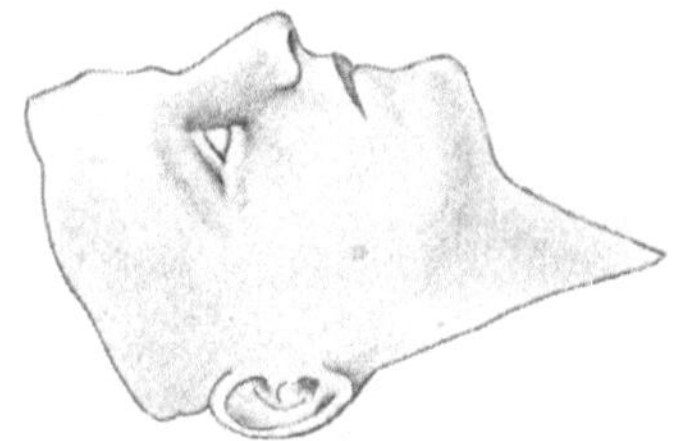

11

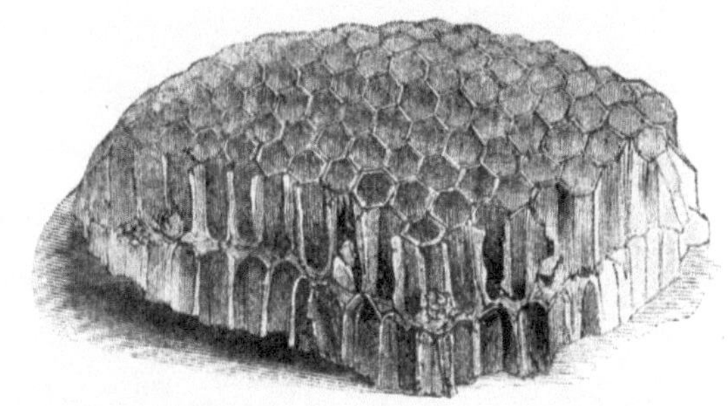

12

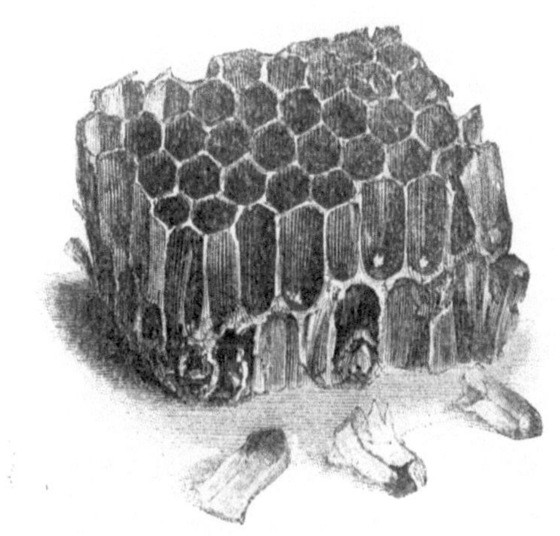

13

11. Wax mask 12. New comb

13 Comb in which bees have been bred, showing the cocoons

PLATE VII.

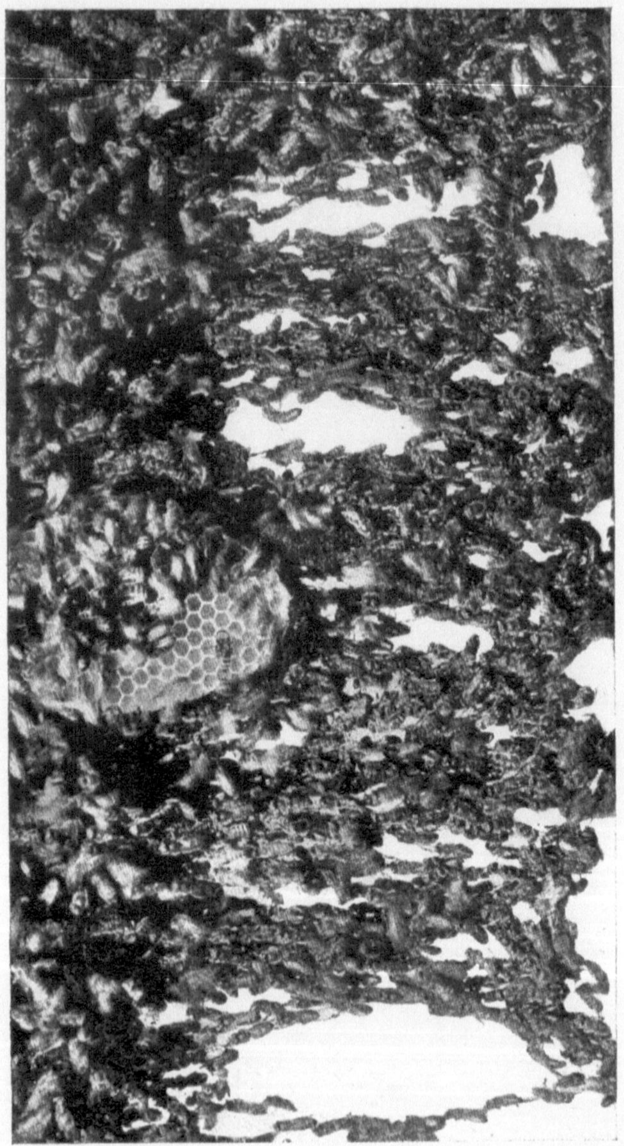

14. Bees clustering in comb-building.

to be masticated by the jaws with the addition of saliva, which modifies the wax and makes it plastic. Dr. de Planta found a considerable quantity of saliva in the wax when prepared for use in comb-building, while in the scales it was certainly absent.

Huber, after a series of experiments—several times repeated—proved that bees fed on honey and water produced wax, while, if fed only on pollen, none was produced. He also showed that bees fed on sugar-syrup were able to produce wax, and (after several consecutive trials) that those fed with syrup made of sugar yielded more wax than when fed on honey, brown moist sugar yielding the largest quantities. These results were fully corroborated by Dumas and Milne-Edwards, who in 1844 repeated Huber's experiments, and found that 500 grammes of sugar yielded 30 grammes of wax, while the same quantity of honey only gave 20 grammes. Other observers, such as Gundelach and Berlepsch, have obtained similar results, so that Huber's conclusions may be considered as established.

Although honey or saccharine matter alone is needed, Berlepsch and others have pointed out that bees cannot do without pollen, which serves to make up for the enormous wear-and-tear of tissue caused by wax-secretion. The elaboration of wax not only draws largely on the vital powers of the bee, but also costs both bees and their owners much honey. The exact amount of honey consumed in producing a given quantity of wax has not yet been definitely decided, scientists differing so widely in their opinions as to vary between 6½ lb. and 20 lb. of honey being required for 1 lb. of wax, without counting loss of time caused in the building of combs. Taking the average at 13¼ lb., and comparing the value of honey to that of wax, it will be seen that the loss is considerable.

Beeswax, when pure, though usually pale yellow in colour, is sometimes nearly white, and the difference in colour is due, as Dr. de Planta has pointed out, to pollen consumed by the bees. For instance, when bees are collecting pollen and honey from heather, the pollen being white, the wax is also white, whereas, when collecting from sainfoin, the pollen being orange-coloured, the wax also partakes of this colour.

According to Brande, wax is composed of 80.20 per cent. carbon, 13.14 hydrogen, and 6.36 oxygen.

Its specific gravity is between .960 and .967, and it melts at about 143 deg. to 147 deg. Fahr. At 85 deg. it becomes plastic, and is then readily moulded and kneaded into shape.

Sir Benjamin Brodie in 1848 demonstrated that beeswax mainly consisted of *cerotic acid* ($C_{27}H_{57}O_2$), *myricine* or *palmitate of myricyle* ($C_{16}H_{31}O$, $C_{30}H_{61}O$), and a small quantity of a fatty substance resembling margarine, to which Lewy gave the name *ceroleine.* Otto Hehner, who submitted to analysis a large number of samples of English and foreign wax, found it remarkably constant in composition. Cerotic acid he found to vary only from 13 to 16 per cent., and the quantity of myricine from 86 to 89 per cent. This includes 4 to 5 per cent. of ceroleine.

By boiling wax in alcohol the myricine separates; as the alcohol cools the cerotic acid crystallises out, leaving ceroleine in solution.

Beeswax is soluble in ether, chloroform, benzol, bisulphide of carbon, turpentine, &c.; partially soluble in boiling alcohol; and insoluble in water or cold alcohol.

During the process of bleaching, wax parts with 1 per cent. of carbon, and absorbs 1 per cent. of oxygen. The cerotic acid from bleached wax contains more oxygen and less carbon than that obtained from unbleached wax, whereas the myricine in either remains the same. Hehner says he has "every reason to believe that the changes due to some of the bleaching processes alter the composition of the wax more deeply than is generally supposed."

Besides beeswax, there are in commerce wax from plants and other insects than bees, and mineral wax. Of these we shall have to speak later, some of them being used for adulterating beeswax.

The beeswax of commerce is found in cakes of different sizes and shapes, varying in colour from light to dark yellow. It breaks with a fine-grained, clean conchoidal fracture, has more or less aroma, is plastic, tenacious, and can be kneaded without its sticking to the fingers. Placed in the mouth it is nearly tasteless, and when chewed does not adhere to the teeth.

Beeswax retains its ductility and tenacity under greater ranges of temperature than any mineral, plant, or insect wax, and is therefore the only one suitable for making comb-foundation (Fig. 18, Plate VIII.); not only so, but it has been found that an admixture of 25 to 50 per cent. of paraffin or ceresin is very liable to melt down in hot weather. Practically, therefore, pure beeswax is the only product that should be used in making foundation for use in hives.

PLATE VIII.

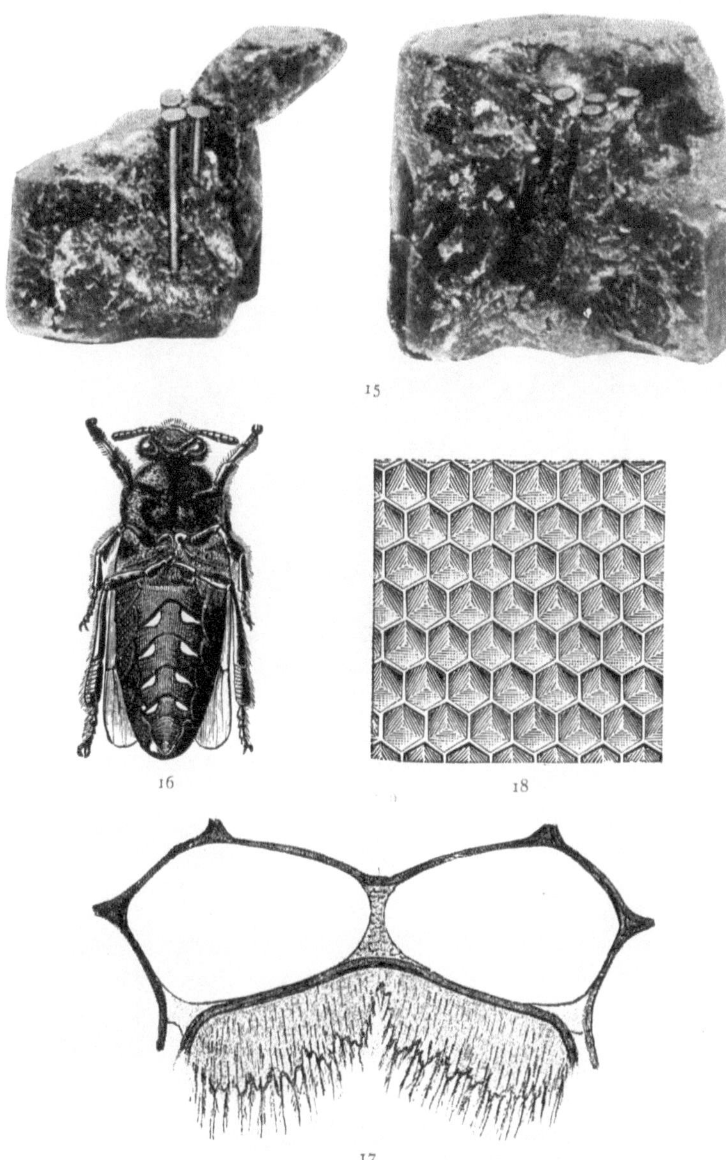

15. Wax adulterated by the insertion of nails.
16. Bee, showing wax-scales on abdomen
17. Ventral plate of worker
18. Comb-foundation

PLATE IX.

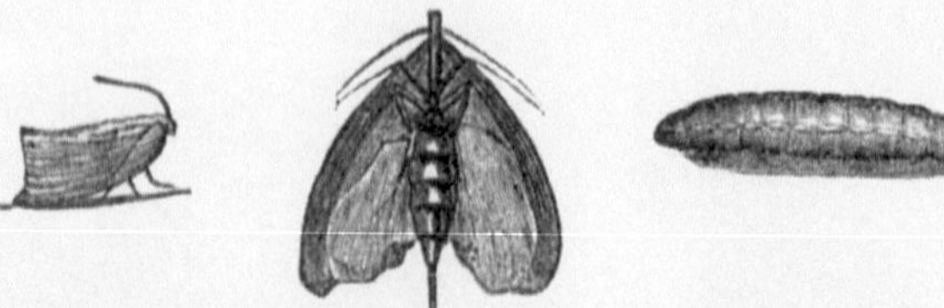

19

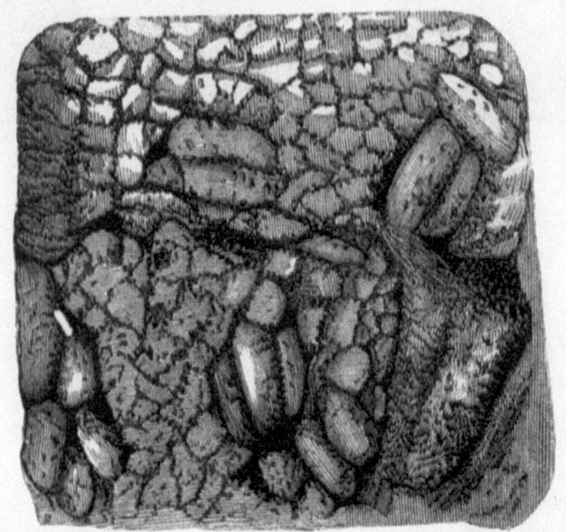

20

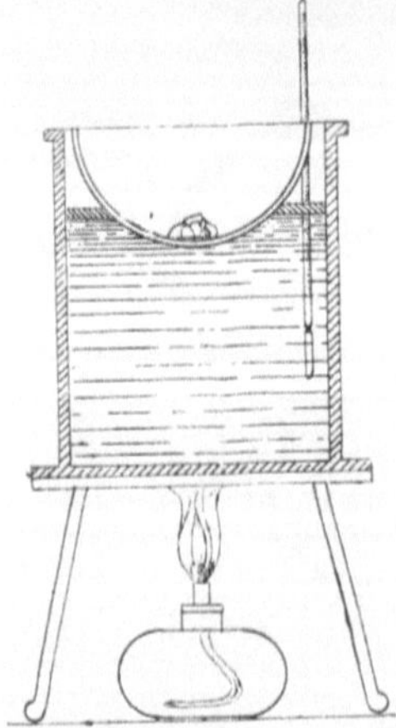

21

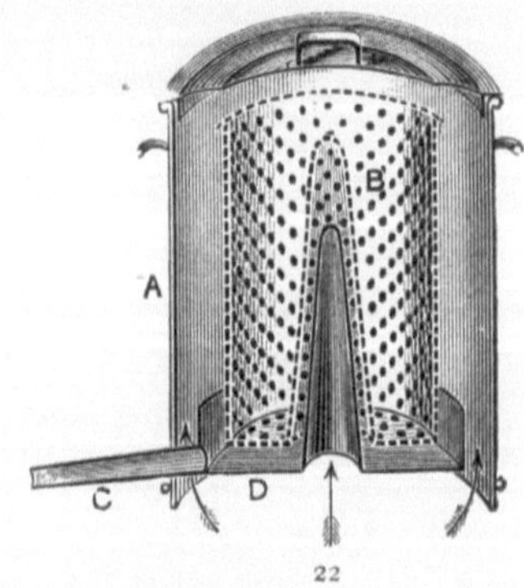

22

19 Wax-moth (Galleria cerella).
20 Combs destroyed by wax-moth.
21. Appliance for testing melting-point of wax
22 Gerster's wax-extractor

Chapter III.

WAX RENDERING.

SOME of the primitive methods of separating wax from its impurities were extremely crude; even now the natives of different countries from which we obtain wax are most careless in its preparation, so that the imported article when put on the market here is not seldom full of foreign substances.

The common practice is to break up the combs and strain the honey from them, after which they are placed in a cauldron of water. As the combs generally contain pollen and brood, they are allowed to soak for a time in order to soften the pollen and cast off skins of the cocoons. A fire is then lighted under the cauldron and the mass boiled, being stirred meanwhile with a stick to cause the combs to go to pieces. When the wax is all melted that which floats on the top is ladled out on to a canvas or other strainer placed over a pan containing a little water. More combs are put into the cauldron, and the process continued so long as there are any combs to melt. When cool enough the refuse is squeezed with the hands to remove what wax remains, the débris being thrown away. But a good deal of pollen with small particles of rubbish passes through the strainer. In dealing with best samples the wax is re-melted in clean water and strained again. This method is a very wasteful one, it being impossible to impart sufficient pressure by squeezing to extract all the wax, consequently a good deal is thrown away with the refuse. The crude method described also frequently ends in the wax becoming discoloured from burning.

A better plan, that of boiling in bags, will be described later, being one still extensively adopted by those who have not taken to modern methods.

Formerly the production of wax was much greater than now. Modern bee-keeping does not yield so much wax as is obtained when bees are kept in skeps or boxes, or by any of the primitive methods by which the great majority of stocks are destroyed annually and all combs melted for wax. On the other hand, the bee-keeper who works with movable-comb hives extracts the honey and returns the combs to be refilled. In this case the only wax obtained is from comb-cappings, removed previous to extracting the honey. He may, of course, have sundry pieces of combs that have become too old for use, and which he may desire to renew, cut out from his frames along with combs from skeps from which bees have been driven, and, as beeswax is of considerable value and readily saleable, every scrap of comb should be carefully preserved for melting.

Comb-cappings and any pieces of comb in which no brood has been reared (Fig. 12, Plate VI.) should have a separate melting, as needing far less refining than combs which have contained brood and pollen (Fig. 13, Plate VI.).

When combs intended for melting have contained honey, this should be washed out of them, and if they are not intended to be melted at once should be broken up and kneaded into solid balls, pressing out all the water. These balls can then be dried and put away for subsequent melting. They should be kept together in a dry place along with any other pieces of comb, carefully preserved from wax-moth, which is particularly troublesome during the summer months. The larva of the wax-moth (*Galleria cerella*) (Fig. 19, Plate IX.) eats the wax, fills the combs with cocoons, and, if not stopped in time, will destroy the greater part of the wax and leave nothing but a mass of entangled silky webs and débris extending in all directions (Fig. 20, Plate IX.).

All wax should be carefully preserved in a case or cupboard capable of being tightly closed, and in which sulphur should be burnt from time to time. Sulphur fumes destroy the eggs and larvæ of the moth.

Many different methods are employed for separating wax from its impurities, all of which plans are based on the fact that beeswax melts at a temperature of 143 deg. Fahr., when it readily separates from such foreign substances as it may contain by reason of its lighter specific gravity.

The melting of combs can be done either by the heat of the sun's rays, or with boiling water, or by steam. But only rain or river water is suitable for the purpose, and no other should be used, seeing that well-water, if hard, is liable to cause wax to turn brown in colour. Lime in water also unites with the fatty acid of wax, saponifying it, so that, after cooling, wax rendered with hard water has on the under side a spongy, greyish mass. When rain or river water is not available, vinegar or a small quantity of sulphuric acid should be put into the water, just sufficient to neutralise the lime.

Copper vessels are preferable, but if not available, iron ones can be used, but they should be first heated and rubbed with a piece of mutton fat, which not only prevents the acid from attacking the iron, but the latter will not afterwards discolour the wax. It should also be noted that the nearer to the melting-point at which all melting operations are performed the finer will be the product, a high temperature destroying both the colour and aroma of the wax produced.

The methods usually employed for rendering wax may be divided into three classes:—

1. Those depending only upon heat.
2. Those employing both water and heat.
3. Those dependent on presses and hot water.

We will now describe the various ways of extracting wax from the combs and the different appliances used.

The Solar Wax-Extractor.—This appliance is only suitable for melting the wax from new combs or from cappings. Such combs as have been used for brood-rearing and are very old contain many generations of cocoons (Fig 13, Plate VI.), consequently very little wax, if any, can be got from them by means of a solar extractor. It can, however, be usefully employed for clarifying wax obtained by any of the other mentioned processes and which is already in the form of wax-cakes. But although the solar extractor will only work during sunshine, every bee-keeper should possess one. It is extremely handy for holding any piece of comb cut out when manipulating among bees, and, left to itself, the wax is melted without any trouble to the bee-keeper. The appliance consists of a wooden box with a double glazed frame sloping from back to front (Fig. 23, Plate X.). A slightly inclined tin tray fits inside, and on this the combs or pieces of wax are laid. If the apparatus is now placed in the sun, so that the rays strike the sloping glass, the wax will melt and run quite pure into the receptacle in front of the tray, leaving nothing but the residue behind on the wire gauze.

It has been found, by means of a thermometer fixed inside the case, that the wax began to melt when the temperature reached 147 deg. to 149 deg. Fahr., and on rising to between 161 deg. and 172 deg. the molten wax flowed rapidly.

Dr. Bianchetti carried out a number of experiments in this line, and found that with a shade temperature of 69.8 deg. Fahr. at

PLATE X.

23

24

23. Solar wax extractor
24. The "Hatch-Gemmil" wax-press.

PLATE XI.

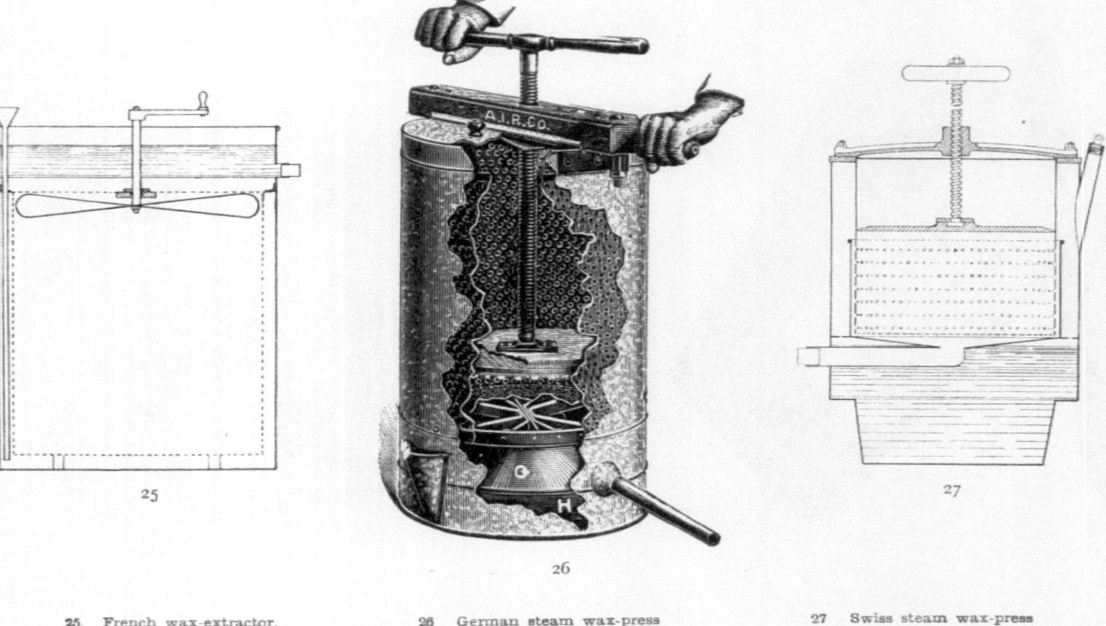

25. French wax-extractor.

26 German steam wax-press

27 Swiss steam wax-press

midday the thermometer in the solar wax-extractor registered 140 deg. at 9 a.m., 172.4 deg. at 11 a.m., 186.8 deg. at noon, and 165.2 deg. at 4 p.m.

Wax obtained by means of this apparatus is very fine and requires no further refining.

Extracting in an Oven.—Some have advocated melting small quantities of combs in an oven; but this plan cannot be recommended, because if the heat of the oven be too great the wax is not only volatilised, but becomes brown and acquires a disagreeable odour that reduces its marketable value. If, however, it is decided to use this method care should be taken that the oven does not become too hot. In no case should the temperature exceed 172 deg. Fahr. The pieces of comb are put into a sieve or wire-gauze strainer placed in a basin containing water, and in due course the molten wax percolates through the strainer and drops into the water, on which it floats. When all is melted the contents are allowed to cool gradually, when the cake of wax can be removed. This plan, like the solar, is also unsuitable for old combs, for the same reasons.

Extracting with Hot Water.—This way of rendering wax is extensively adopted by bee-keepers who are still working on old methods in places where wax is obtained in large quantities. The combs are pressed to rid them of the honey, then thoroughly soaked in water for twenty-four hours, and afterwards put into canvas bags and boiled in a copper or other vessel of water. Brood-combs are sometimes served in the same way in order to get all the wax possible out of them. The object of soaking is to impregnate with water the skins of the cocoons (Fig. 13, Plate VI.), which would otherwise absorb the wax as it became melted. The larval excrement will also dissolve in the water and discolour it. The bags are kept floating below the surface of the water by weighting down with stones, some of which are so placed as to prevent the bags from touching the bottom of the copper. Heat is then applied, the wax melts, percolates through the canvas, and floats to the top. The water is only allowed to boil very gently, and the boiling must be continued for from a quarter of to half an hour, according to the amount of refuse there is in the wax. Great care is taken not to boil too fast or the wax will rise like milk or become over-heated, and if this happens it becomes dry, brittle, and brown—an objectionable colour, almost impossible to get rid of. When most of the wax has been extracted the bag is removed and pressed between two boards, thus securing what wax may be squeezed from the refuse. The scum is then taken off, the copper covered over with cloths, and the water and wax are allowed to cool as slowly as possible, for the slower in cooling the more refined the wax becomes, and, consequently, increases in value. When cold, the cake of wax is taken out, the discoloured portion adhering to the under side scraped off, and, after re-melting a second time, it is cast into round cakes. The refuse that is scraped off is collected, and when there is a sufficient quantity of it the same process is gone through and the last trace of clean wax removed.

Another way is to put the combs into the copper, and a hoop just fitting within, covered with canvas or cheese-cloth, is pressed down over the combs. The hoop is prevented from rising by sticks wedged against the ceiling; this done, the copper is filled with rain-water, the fire lighted, and, upon boiling, the wax rises through the canvas to the surface, leaving the refuse behind. The cooling process is the same as that followed in the previous method.

There are several wax-extractors on the market by means of which brood-combs are disintegrated in boiling water. A French one, an improved form of which is shown in Fig. 25, Plate XI., is very simple, and consists of an outer cylindrical kettle, inside which is a basket of perforated tin resting on small supports to keep it off the bottom of the kettle, and having a top of tinned-wire gauze stretched over and fixed to an iron hoop, which fits into the basket, and is kept down by means of two catches. This has a bar across in which the spindle carrying two fans revolves. Near the top of the kettle is an outlet for the wax, closed by means of a cork, and on the opposite side a funnel reaches nearly down to the bottom. The basket, after being filled with combs and the gauze top is fitted on, is then put into the kettle and kept in its place by means of two stops. The kettle is next filled with water saturated with common salt until it reaches a little higher than the wax outlet. This done, it is put on the fire and allowed to boil, while the crank at the end of the spindle is turned from time to time to thoroughly break up the combs under the hot water, so that the wax is liberated and rises to the surface. When all the wax is supposed to be extracted the cork may be removed from the spout and the wax allowed to flow into a receptacle containing a little warm water. Some hot salt-water is then poured in at the funnel until the last drop of wax has escaped, when the cage can be taken out, emptied, refilled, and the operation repeated, making use of the same hot water.

Extracting by Steam.—For this purpose some use the wax-extractor devised by Professor Gerster, shown in Fig. 22, Plate IX. It consists of an outer tin cylinder (A) having a dish (D) inside, communicating with the outlet (C). Between this dish and the outer cylinder is a space which allows the steam to pass up to the basket, and a tube up the centre of the basket serves the same purpose. The perforated tin basket (B) stands about an inch from the bottom of the dish. When working, the basket, filled with comb, is inserted in cylinder (A). The whole is then placed over a pan containing water on the fire. When the water boils steam passes through the openings in the direction shown by arrows and melts the wax, which oozes through the perforations in the basket into the dish and then runs from spout (C) into a basin of water, leaving the refuse in basket (B). Wax extracted by this method is free from impurities and of a beautiful colour, but it is only suited for new combs or cappings. The latter can be put into the wax-extractor when extracting, the honey drained from them, and when the basket is full the wax may be melted.

Wax-Presses.—By far the most satisfactory plan, and one that now obtains extensively with advanced bee-keepers, is to use some form of wax-press, in which the pressure brought to bear, combined with heat, removes the wax without leaving more than from 1 to 3 per cent. in the refuse.

Wax-presses may be divided into two classes: those in which heat is either applied during the pressure or the contrary, according to the one chosen.

The first-named of the heated presses is also made in two forms, one where great pressure is applied to combs in hot water and another where steam only is used. In such appliances the pressure can be continued without danger of cooling the combs and the pressure released in order to allow the combs to be again saturated with the boiling water or steam. The pressure is then re-applied and the operation repeated until all the wax has been removed.

With all the various presses we are now about to describe it is advantageous to mingle with the combs a certain quantity of straw, preferably rye-straw, cut into lengths of about two inches, as tending to make the mass more porous and facilitate the flowing of the molten wax.

Hot-water Press.—This consists of an iron cylinder with a spout near the top and a funnel at the side. Inside the vessel are several division-racks, between which are placed canvas bags containing the combs. On the bottom is a coarse grating, over which is a wire screen, so placed as to prevent the bags from being pressed through and keep them from touching the bottom. At the top there is a flat board, and pressure is applied by means of a screw. When using the extractor the grating is placed in position, and one of the bags of comb laid on it, and a division-rack between every bag, two or three of which are generally used at the same time. The combs should have been soaked in water previous to tying up in the bags. When as many layers as will nearly fill the cylinder have been put in, the flat board mentioned is placed on the top, the bar carrying the screw adjusted, and the vessel filled with water by means of the funnel at the side until it begins to run out of the spout. The whole is then put on the fire and allowed to boil, pressure being applied by turning the screw, when the wax is forced through the canvas and floats on the top of the water. More hot water is introduced as required, and causes the melted wax to overflow through the outlet. The screw is then turned in the opposite direction so that the mass is relieved of pressure, and it becomes again saturated with boiling water.

Owing to the continued high temperature the colour of wax from such presses is not very good, but if hot water is introduced frequently so that the wax can be run off at short intervals this difficulty is overcome and the colour is unimpaired.

The pressure in every case should be intermittent, it being found that more wax can be extracted from old combs than by continuous steady pressure. Messrs. Root, who have had great experience with such presses, say that old combs may be pressed as many as fifteen or twenty times, rendering it possible to reduce the final loss of wax to a fraction of 1 per cent.

STEAM PRESS.—Methods of applying pressure to combs permeated with steam have also been in use for a long time, and although such presses have the advantage that the wax drops down out of the way as soon as it leaves the refuse, the quality is not so good owing to the high temperature to which it is subjected.

One of the most popular is that known as the German steam press. Fig. 26, Plate XI., illustrates one as now made by the A. I. Root Company. Steam, generated in the compartment (H), rises through an opening in the false bottom (G), and surrounds the comb beneath the plunger in the perforated metal basket. The wax as it oozes through this runs down on to the conical false bottom and passes out of the spout. In working the press the can is first put on the fire, so that the water may become heated while the perforated basket is being filled to about 8 in. or 10 in. in depth with old combs previously soaked in water and put into a canvas bag. Instead of putting all the comb into one bag, it is preferable to have two or three, with circular boards between each layer. The basket is then placed in the can and the screw turned up as far as it will go in the cross-arm, which is locked in position by turning it until the bolts catch in the ears at the sides. As soon as steam is generated it will rise, thoroughly heat the comb, and the molten wax runs out of the spout at the bottom. When the wax stops running pressure is applied by turning the screw, very slowly at first, and increasing the pressure by degrees. When the screw is down as far as it will go it is turned back, the cross-bar taken out, and the contents of the bags shaken up previous to being subjected to renewed steaming and pressure, two or three repeats being necessary to secure thorough work.

A Swiss appliance working on the same principle is shown in Fig. 27, Plate XI. It consists of an outer vessel containing an inner one with a conical bottom and an outlet tube. A perforated cylinder is supported by means of a flange on the top edge of the outer vessel. This is closed at the top with a strong iron cover, fixed by means of four screws. Through the cover passes a screw, having a wheel on the end, which when turned moves the plunger up or down. The funnel at the side is for supplying the vessel with water. The combs are treated as explained above and a bag containing them placed in the perforated cylinder. Steam passes through holes between the two outer vessels, softens the wax, which can be pressed out by turning the wheel at the top, and the molten wax then runs from the tube.

The same objection applies to steam presses as to steam extractors, the best methods by far being those in which unheated presses are used.

Unheated Press.—With this press neither hot water nor steam surrounds the comb while pressure is being applied, but the comb is

PLATE XII.

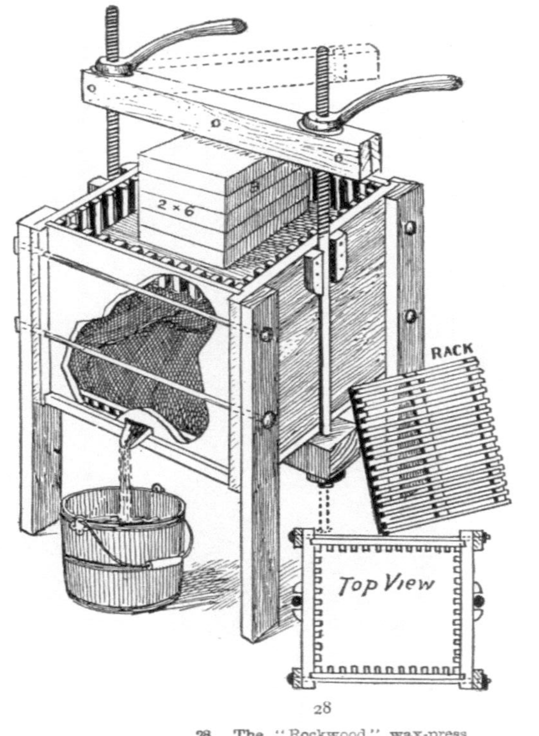

28

28 The "Rockwood" wax-press

29

29. Root's wax-press, showing different parts.

PLATE XIII.

30

30. Root's wax-press, ready for receiving wax

31

31 The same press in operation

previously heated, and is pressed without additional heat during the operation. It is melted with boiling water and then dipped into the press, the latter being lined with canvas. This material is then folded over carefully and the pressure applied by means of a screw. The work must be done expeditiously in order to prevent the wax from getting chilled. Fig. 24, Plate X., shows the "Hatch-Gemmil" press, and sufficiently explains itself. It is made of wood—as being best for retaining heat—and is generally filled with boiling water to warm it just before using, otherwise much of the wax becomes chilled and adheres to the sides of the press.

Another form of press, known as the "Rockwood," is shown in Fig. 28, Plate XII.

A press somewhat different in design and perfected by Messrs. Root is shown in Figs. 29, 30, and 31, Plates XII. and XIII. By reference to Fig. 29, Plate XII., it will be seen that, instead of having a square wooden box, a round can, constructed of tin, is used. A heavy wire-cloth or perforated-metal lining, made rather smaller than the outer can, is placed inside this. Messrs. Root now prefer to use vertical wooden cleats in lieu of the perforated-metal lining, as they provide a freer exit for the wax. The round form of can is much stronger than a square box, which tends to bulge out when pressure is applied, thus bursting the canvas. Being more compact, the mass is also less liable to chill. The screw extends downwards into a hole in the centre of the cast-iron follower, and thus prevents the latter from going down sideways, in which case the pressure would be distributed unevenly and more wax remain in the thick part than in the thinner. The circular wooden follower is cleated, and this assists the wax and water in flowing off. Since no heat is applied to the combs during the pressing, it is advisable to do the extracting in warm weather or in a room that can be heated by means of a stove in order to avoid chilling the wax and thus hindering the work. The boiler used for melting the combs is placed on the stove, and the press should stand as near to it as possible to avoid "drip" when the melted comb is being dipped from the boiler into it.

When ready for work put water in the boiler, and when it begins to boil immerse the combs by degrees, stirring frequently and taking care not to add too much comb in proportion to the water, the best results being obtained when there is plenty of the latter. Keep stirring until no lumps remain and the combs have been reduced to a mash. A wooden plug is placed in the spout at the bottom of the wax-press can, and, after putting therein the follower and canvas sacking, heat the press thoroughly by filling it with boiling water to prevent the mass from becoming chilled. The water is then drawn off by removing the plug, the can being drawn forward, and the canvas spread over it, as seen in Fig. 30, Plate XIII. About a gallon of melted comb and water is dipped out of the boiler into the press and the canvas folded over it. The latter should be about a foot larger on each side than the press, so that it may fold over neatly and evenly. The cleated follower is next placed on the top, with the cleats running in the direction of the spout, which should also be the position of the cleated board at the bottom. The can is then pushed back under the screw (Fig. 31, Plate XIII.), and pressure applied slowly, turning the screw until no more wax runs out. This point reached, the press is tipped up in order to drain the wax and water from the can, when another turn or two of the screw will squeeze out all that remains in the refuse. When neither wax nor water comes away the screw is turned back, the follower removed, and the whole contents of the canvas put into a receptacle close at hand for after treatment, it having been found that one extracting will only remove from 88 to 92 per cent. of the total amount of wax. When all the melted combs have gone through the first operation the accumulated refuse is returned to the boiler, heated up again, and pressed as before. This takes less time than the first treatment, and only about 1 to 3 per cent. of waste remains.

The whole of the wax and water from the press is then poured into a can and kept covered so as to cool very slowly, thus preventing the wax from cracking and allowing of its removal next day in a solid cake.

The quality of wax obtained from such a press is of the best, and the colour generally so good as to need little or no refining.

Chapter IV.

BEESWAX IN COMMERCE.

BEE-KEEPING is carried on throughout Europe, but the main producers of wax are Germany, Austria-Hungary, France, Russia, Spain, Italy, and Turkey. In these countries many bees are kept, and from the Middle Ages German bee-masters were foremost in the honey and the wax-producing industry. Later on, however, other countries have entered the field, and the New World, with its virgin pastures and the great activity of its inhabitants, has proved a formidable competitor.

Large quantities of beeswax now come from the Orient, the principal countries supplying it being the East Indies, China, and Asiatic Turkey. The West Indies, Australia, Africa, and North and South America also produce wax which finds its way into European markets.

It is generally admitted that the best wax is that collected in England, after which comes that from other parts of Europe, Australia,

Africa, and America, the worst being Gambia wax, while that from Senegal is very dark and has an unpleasant odour. Both the latter come in blocks or cylindrical masses of about 50 lb. weight.

Considerable quantities are also imported from the United States of America, the best of which is shipped from New York. Chile also sends good wax; whereas most of that from South America is of inferior quality and bleaches with difficulty, that from Brazil not bleaching at all.

Germany has always produced a much-prized wax for technical, medicinal, and artistic uses, but, although some of this finds its way into other markets, most of it is used in the country where produced, manufactured articles chiefly being exported.

Excellent wax is found in the markets of Austria-Hungary and Switzerland, but Turkey is said to produce wax of finer quality than any of those named, great care being taken in its preparation. It is of a bright orange-red colour and fetches the highest price on the market. That from Greece is nearly as good. In France bee-keeping is carried on extensively, Brittany and the South producing the best wax of that country; but none of this gets into foreign markets, being exclusively used in the country where obtained, a certain additional quantity being imported in order to supply the whole demand. In Paris quite a number of firms deal exclusively in wax and honey, and there are also many wax-bleaching factories employing several hundreds of workmen. Closely following the French we have Spanish wax, which comes in cakes of from 2 lb. to 3 lb. in weight. Italy also produces a considerable quantity of excellent wax, and manages to export some, notwithstanding the large amount used in that country for religious and other purposes.

In Russia the peasants use honey extensively instead of sugar, and the churches make a heavy demand on wax for tapers. It is said that in the Government of Ekaterinoslav there are nearly four hives to every inhabitant, so that the production of wax there must be enormous. From other than European countries we have wax from Egypt and Morocco, large quantities of good quality, but full of impurities, being shipped from Mogador. Excellent wax also comes from Abyssinia, Zanzibar, and Madagascar, that from the last-named place having a pleasant aromatic odour. The islands of the Indian Archipelago, Timor, Timor-Laut, and Flores export annually about 20,000 piculs of wax in Portuguese vessels to China, where also large quantities of wax are obtained, but not sufficient for the requirements of the country.

Apis dorsata, the famous and fierce wild honey-bee of India, builds an enormous single comb, sometimes 5 ft. or 6 ft. long, usually in inaccessible places. The wax, of excellent quality, is eagerly sought after, in spite of the difficulty and danger in securing it. One comb is said to yield from 1 lb. to 1½ lb. of wax.

Wax from the West Indian Islands varies much in colour and quality, the best coming from Hayti, though this is hard and nearly black; that from Jamaica is also highly esteemed. A very dark wax, which cannot be bleached, comes from Guadeloupe. It is obtained from wild bees and contains much earthy matter.

Beeswax forms a considerable part of the cargoes of ships trading to the Gold and Ivory Coasts and districts of Sierra Leone and the western shores of Africa, a very small quantity coming to us from the Niger.

Wax differs much not only in colour, but in the amount of impurities it contains, the natives in some countries being very careless in their preparation of it for market. This fault regulates the price, which varies from £6 to £8 per cwt., wholesale.

The following are some of the places from which come the supplies to the London and Liverpool markets, showing the principal waxes and their respective colours:—

Places whence Imported.	*Colour of Wax.*
Abyssinia	Pale yellow to orange.
Australia	Grey, nearly white, and pale yellow to light orange. Some is of a dirty yellow and contains a certain admixture of grease.
Brazil	Mahogany colour.
Chile	Bright yellow.
East Indies	Yellow, contains as much as 7 per cent. of impurities.
France	Bright orange.
Gambia	Dark brown.
Hayti	Nearly black, hard, with aromatic odour.
Jamaica	Bright yellow to dark brown.
Madagascar	Light brown, aromatic odour.
Mauritius	Light to dark brown.
Mombassa	Light yellow to dark orange.
Niger	Grey, yellow to dark brown.
Senegal	Dark brown, unpleasant odour.
Turkey	Bright orange-red.
United States of America	Yellow to brown, greenish-white, very variable in colour and aroma.

CHAPTER V.

REFINING AND BLEACHING WAX.

THE colour of beeswax obtained from melting combs varies from pale yellow to brown, and when procured from bee-keepers working on modern principles is pretty free from impurities. But much of the wax dealt with in ordinary commerce comes from countries where modern methods are unknown, and where the natives use primitive means of preparing it for market, consequently imported wax contains many impurities, which have to be got rid of before it can be used.

For many manufacturing purposes colour is of little importance, and the imported article can be used after eliminating its impurities. Certain industries, however, require a white wax, and bleaching is therefore necessary in order to remove all colouring matter from the commercial product. It is also notable that different kinds of wax bleach with differing degrees of facility; thus the waxes of England, Hamburg, Odessa, Portugal, Mogador,

Zanzibar, East and West Indies, and North America all bleach very rapidly, while those of Cuba, Danzig, Königsberg, Gaboon, and Gambia can only be bleached with difficulty, and it is found impossible to bleach the soft, mahogany-coloured wax of the Brazils at all.

The refining and bleaching of wax was at one time carried on as an independent trade, the extent of which may be gauged from the fact that towards the end of the seventeenth century there were in Hamburg alone fourteen bleaching-houses. The introduction in later years of vegetable and mineral substitutes for beeswax has considerably lessened the trade, yet wax-bleaching is still an important industry both in Europe and in America.

Chemical processes, as a rule, more or less injure wax. All bleaching is, therefore, done in the open air by subjecting it to the rays of the sun, the factories being usually situated in country places far removed from the contaminating influence of smoke and other impurities, it being found that the process of bleaching cannot be carried on in towns, where the air is charged with dust and tarry soot, which clings to the wax and gives it a brown tint impossible to remove.

TESTING COMMERCIAL WAX.—Wax, as imported, is received at the bleaching factories in cakes of all sizes and colours, therefore before these are mixed each sample is tested to ascertain its bleaching capacity, and, it being necessary to make these tests as rapidly as possible, chemicals are employed. For this purpose a solution is prepared by adding 1 part of fresh chloride of lime to 10 parts of water, stirring this well in order thoroughly to blend the two. The solution is then passed through filtering-paper. This operation should be performed as rapidly as possible so that the chlorine (the active agent in bleaching) should not volatilise and thus be lost.

The sample of wax to be tested is first cut into thin flakes, which are placed in a glass-stoppered bottle, and some of the clear solution mentioned above poured on them; the stopper is then replaced and the whole well shaken. If it becomes white in from five to seven minutes, the wax may be classed among those bleaching rapidly. Each sample is tested separately, and the time occupied in bleaching noted on the label, in order that some idea may be formed of the time required in the longer process of bleaching by sunlight. The wax is then assorted in accordance with these results, the cakes of equal bleaching capacity being mixed. This done, the process of refining to eliminate impurities is commenced.

REFINING WAX.—In this process the melting is done in water at a low temperature, and the more frequent the meltings the cleaner the wax becomes, the colour separating along with the impurities. Some factories use steam for the purpose, and under its influence wax is cleaned and filtered, thus avoiding a great deal of the after manipulation entailed in the first-named method.

Steam apparatus in which wax is melted are either jacketed or have a spiral tube within the tank through which the steam passes, and in this way water can be kept at an even temperature. The filters are also double-walled, the steam passing between the walls, the smallest impurities being thus removed.

Some refiners in melting wax use a small quantity of sulphuric acid, and thus facilitate the separation of certain impurities, which subside in the acidulated water. The wax is cut by machinery into very small shavings, and in this condition is put into a vat with water, a little concentrated sulphuric acid being added—the proportion of acid is one pint to a ton of wax. Steam is then blown into the vat by means of a coiled pipe pierced with holes, the mixture meanwhile being kept in constant agitation. After a time it is covered over with cloths and allowed to stand quiet, when the impurities subside to the bottom and the wax floats to the surface as a clear and almost colourless liquid.

The A. I. Root Company, of Medina, Ohio, who manufacture an enormous quantity of comb-foundation yearly, use sulphuric acid. For this purpose they employ a wooden tank a little over 3½ ft. in diameter and about 5 ft. high, and describe in their latest "A B C" book the method of procedure in the following words:—"Water is run into it to a depth of 12 in., and then 1,500 lb. of wax is thrown in, making it about full. The mass is then heated by means of a jet of steam from a pipe projecting down into the water from the top. When all the wax is melted the acid is poured in. If all the wax is so dark as to make brood-foundation, seven pints of acid are used; but if light enough to make super-foundation, not more than three quarts are used. If the wax is already of good quality, so small an amount as two quarts of acid will answer. On an average, therefore, we use three quarts of acid to eighty gallons of water for 1,500 lb. of wax. Soon after this is poured in the colour of the boiling wax will be seen to grow lighter, and after a minute or so the boiling is stopped. The steam-pipe is now drawn out and the tank covered with a cloth or carpet, and allowed to stand as many hours as the wax will remain liquid, or about twenty-four hours. At the expiration of this time the water and acid will have settled to the bottom by reason of their greater specific gravity, and the acid, in turn, having a greater specific gravity than the water, will settle to the bottom of the water, and the consequence is that the wax itself, after being purified, is allowed to become thoroughly cleansed of any residue of acid, and the dirt accumulation will all have settled to the bottom of the wax and into the water. The melted wax is now drawn off from the top and poured into any sort of receptacle with flaring sides. When the wax is nearly to the bottom, or when it shows evidence of coming near the dirt, the rest is allowed to stand. As soon as it is caked in the tank it is lifted out, and the dirt clinging to the bottom scraped off."

Where steam is not used the melting is done by putting the wax, broken into small pieces, in a tinned copper with water, to every gallon of which 1½ oz. of sulphuric acid is added. This is heated, and the mass constantly stirred with a wooden stick, in order that the wax may be thoroughly blended with the water. It is then kept for two hours at a temperature of 158 deg. Fahr., when the firing is stopped, the copper covered over, and the mass allowed to cool very slowly. In this way some of the impurities go to the lower side of the wax, the remainder being precipitated to the bottom of the copper. When cold, the cake of wax is removed and the impure portion of the under side scraped off, after which the cakes are melted again. The water used in melting is then passed through a canvas filter, as particles of wax still adhere to the impurities. These are again melted until the last trace of wax is removed, the refuse being ultimately burnt or used as manure.

Some factories expedite the refining process by adding tartar and borax to the water, the proportion being 50 parts (by weight) of water and 40 of wax to 1 of refined tartar and ½ of borax. The tartar and borax are first dissolved in the water, the wax being then put into it.

It is important to notice that in melting and manipulating wax, if the tanks or kettles are of copper, they must be tinned, or if of iron, they should be enamelled. The verdigris from copper gives a green tint to wax, while iron imparts a reddish tint from the oxide of iron, both elements spoiling the wax for bleaching purposes.

In France, where the preparation of wax is an important industry, about 4 oz. of cream of tartar or alum is added to the water in the first melting copper. The whole is then left for some time, after which the supernatant wax is run off into a settling cistern, whence it is discharged by a tap into moulds, or used for making into strips for bleaching.

After going through any of the processes mentioned, the wax comes out bright yellow in colour, and in this condition is suited for making comb-foundation and a number of other purposes.

BLEACHING WAX.—When a fine, white wax is required the usual way of bleaching is by means of light, the colouring matter being destroyed under the influence of the sun's rays. In practice the wax is cut into thin shavings, so as to expose as much surface as possible to the action of air and light, the latter being the principal agent in the operation.

The refined wax-cakes are broken up, put into a vat, and melted by means of steam. The liquid is then run into an oblong trough called a cradle, which has in the bottom a line of holes, each about the size of a quill. There is also a strainer to prevent any particles of dirt from passing through. This trough is placed over a horizontal drum or wooden cylinder which revolves half-immersed in cold water, a current of this constantly passing through the tank to keep the water cool. The melted wax, running in small streams upon the revolving wet drum, is floated off upon the surface of the water in the form of exceedingly thin strips called ribbons. These are collected at the opposite end of the tank, and, after being drained in baskets, the ribbons of wax are laid upon long webs of canvas stretched horizontally between standards, a couple of feet above the surface of a sheltered field, having a free exposure to the sunbeams. Here they are frequently turned over, then covered by nets to prevent their being blown away by winds, and watered from time to time. Whenever the colour of the wax seems stationary, it is collected, re-melted, and run again into ribbons upon the wet cylinder for the purpose of exposing new surfaces to the blanching operation. After several repetitions of these processes, if the weather proves favourable, the wax eventually loses its yellow tint. The whole operation occupies from ten to sixty days, according to the season, the weather, and the colour of the wax. In Fig. 32, Plate XIV., is

PLATE XIV.

32. Candle-factory and bleaching works.

PLATE XV.

33. "British 'Weed' Foundation Factory

shown the factory and bleaching-yard of Will & Baumer, Syracuse, N.Y., where bleaching on a large scale is carried on.

The bleached wax is finally melted, strained through silk sieves, and then run into circular cavities in a moistened table, to be cast or moulded into thin disc pieces, weighing from 2 oz. to 3 oz. each and measuring 3 in. to 4 in. in diameter.

The wax is not only whitened but hardened in the bleaching process, and its melting-point raised by 1 deg. Fahr. Such wax is white and translucent in thin segments, and has neither taste nor smell. It also loses 1 to 2 per cent. in weight in the process of bleaching.

A common practice in bleaching is to add 1 to 5 per cent. of tallow, which makes yellow wax bleach much more rapidly. The addition of tallow is indispensable when dealing with highly coloured wax, which bleaches with some difficulty and is very brittle, and tallow added in the proportions named is therefore universally allowed, not being considered an adulteration unless more than 5 per cent. is introduced.

In lieu of tallow, 5 to 10 per cent. of essence of turpentine is sometimes employed. As this evaporates in the air and light, the wax bleaches rapidly, and the process can be completed in from ten to fourteen days.

Modern chemistry has shown that bleaching can be rapidly performed with chlorine or other chemical bleaching agents, but these are not generally satisfactory. For instance, wax bleached with chlorine cannot be used for candles, seeing that a chlorine compound is formed, which on burning gives off fumes of hydrochloric acid.

Wax bleached by any chemical process whatever must be thoroughly washed in several changes of water so that not a trace of the chemicals remains, as these would be detrimental to many articles in the manufacture of which the wax is used.

Chapter VI.

ADULTERATION OF WAX.

THERE are few products which undergo so much adulteration as beeswax. Owing to the high price wax realises, dealers are tempted to sophisticate it with a great variety of cheap substances, selected with much skill from those having physical properties similar to wax obtained from bees. Among the adulterants used, paraffins with a high melting-point are chosen; also mineral waxes such as ozokerit, vegetable waxes like Carnauba, and those that come from China and Japan. All these have physical properties resembling beeswax, but their chemical compositions are quite different. The white Chinese and Japanese vegetable waxes are generally used to adulterate bleached wax. In addition to the substances mentioned above, wax may be adulterated with tallow, stearine, resin, mineral powders, kaolin, ochre, chalk, sulphate of baryta, gypsum, and even starch.

Inasmuch as the melting, mixing, and casting

cost something, the adulterations are generally considerable, and it is not unusual to find as much as 50 per cent. or more of these foreign substances mixed with wax.

Apart from what are known as adulterants, we may mention a not very ingenious fraud resorted to by an unscrupulous dealer and shown in Fig. 15, Plate VIII. The wax-cake weighed 1 lb., and the sophisticator had actually forced nails into it and filled up the cavity with melted wax. This, however, was of a different shade from that of the original cake, and the purchaser's attention being naturally drawn to it, the fraud was discovered.

Although the melting-point and specific gravity of the different adulterants vary considerably, these cannot always be relied upon as a test of purity, the skill of adulterators having been carried to such perfection that by mixing different ingredients they are able to produce an imitation that very closely resembles genuine beeswax.

Pure yellow beeswax has a specific gravity of .960 to .963, and tropical waxes may reach .967. The melting-point of yellow wax is about 143 deg. Fahr., whereas that of bleached wax may rise to 156 deg. On the other hand, the melting-point of Chinese insect wax is between 177.8 deg. and 179.6 deg. All vegetable waxes have a much higher specific gravity, ranging between .992 and 1.010, the melting-point being variable. Japanese wax melts between 107 deg. and 113 deg. Fahr., myrtle wax about 115 deg. to 120 deg., palm wax 161 deg., Carnauba wax 185 deg. to 186 deg., purified ceresin melts at 185 deg. to 194 deg., paraffin varies from 100.4 deg. to 176 deg., and tallow from 96 deg. to 122 deg.

From this it will be seen that by various combinations a mixture can be produced very closely resembling beeswax, while not containing a particle of the pure product of the hive. As an instance, Messrs. Buisine mention two French patents described in the *Journal de pharmacie et de chimie* for artificial wax. One consists of a mixture of 2 parts resin and 1 part paraffin, the other being 3 parts resin and 1 part stearic acid.

Mr. Otto Hehner has grouped the several organic substances which may be used as adulterants of wax into three classes:—

1. Acid substances, which embrace the solid, fatty acids, mainly palmitic and stearic, and the acids which constitute resin (practically sylvic acid).
2. Neutral, but saponifiable compounds—viz., stearine and palmitine—of Japan-

ese wax, spermaceti, and Carnauba wax.

3. Paraffin, indifferent to alcoholic potash, is the only marketable product belonging to this class.

Referring to the analysis of the different substances and the possibility of mixing them so as to deceive even the chemist, he says:—"But it is quite easy to imagine mixtures of fatty acids, fat, and paraffin quite devoid of wax, yet giving, on analysis, in the manner proposed, results identical with those yielded by pure wax. Thus a mixture of 9.48 per cent. of fatty acids, 36.84 per cent. of fat, and 53.68 per cent. of paraffin would show on analysis 14.40 per cent. of cerotic acid and 88.09 of myricine." It will be seen, by referring to page 51, that the chemical constituents of this mixture are very similar to those of genuine beeswax.

Paraffin is most frequently used to adulterate beeswax, it being possible to add as much as 20 per cent. of this without sensibly altering the physical properties of the wax. On the other hand, some of the substances mentioned cannot be mixed with beeswax without changing its character considerably, while tallow, stearine, Japanese wax, and Carnauba wax alter its character entirely if the addition exceeds certain limited quantities. Stearine and Japanese wax render it more brittle and less malleable; tallow makes it softer and greasier; Carnauba wax not only makes it harder, but raises the melting-point.

Ceresin, often sold as beeswax, is simply ozokerit (bleached and purified by means of sulphuric acid and distillation), and is used as a substitute for beeswax. It is a mineral wax, which melts at 140 deg. to 149 deg. Fahr., and has nearly the same properties as beeswax. Being obtainable pure white in colour, it resembles bleached wax of the best quality. If a yellow wax is in demand, the imitation article is coloured with gamboge or turmeric, and by adding some aromatic essence even the characteristic odour of beeswax may be fairly imitated.

To test the melting-point of any sample of wax, an apparatus similar to that illustrated in Fig. 21, Plate IX., is used. It consists of a tin vessel standing on a tripod, and has a Wedgwood-ware evaporating dish, on a wire support, for holding the wax. Water is put into the tin, and heated by means of the spirit lamp beneath. A thermometer standing in the water shows the temperature, and when it reaches 143 deg. Fahr. the lamp is removed. If the wax melts before reaching this temperature, adulteration may be suspected, while if a much higher temperature is needed in order to melt the wax, it will probably be adulterated with substances having a high melting-point.

A complete quantitative and qualitative analysis of wax is difficult, and can only be carried out by experts. Dr. A. de Planta, who was an eminent chemist, wrote:—"The adulterations of wax are so difficult to detect that it is scarcely practicable for those who are not experts. Pure beeswax melts at 63.5 C. I have tried the melting-point of twenty-five such pure specimens of beeswax obtained from different countries, and it entirely agreed with that stated above." But since adulteration has been effected with earth-wax, paraffin, and animal fats, the melting-point does not provide sufficient evidence. Otherwise this method would have furnished a good test for those who are not experts.

There remains, therefore, no other way but submitting the wax to a qualified chemist, who will find out the quantity of cerotic acid and non-volatile fatty acids it contains; only an analysis such as this will afford a safe criterion with regard to the adulteration.

We give the following simple tests, which have often been found useful:—

1.—Such inert substances as baryta, ochre, white lead, kaolin, chalk, and gypsum can be detected by melting wax in boiling water, and then thoroughly stirring it; the water becomes clouded, and after allowing it to stand for a short time the solid substances are precipitated.

2.—Another way is to dissolve the wax in ether, benzine, or spirits of turpentine. The solids will then be precipitated, and the amount of adulteration can be judged by the quantity deposited.

3.—Beeswax, when chewed, should afford no unpleasant taste, and it should not stick to the teeth or become pasty, but disintegrate and break up as it is chewed, adulterated wax being cohesive when subjected to the same treatment.

4.—To test the specific gravity, mix in a glass 1 part of alcohol with 2 parts of water. A piece of wax of known purity, and the size of a pea, is then put into this mixture, and, when taken out, pressed between the fingers and replaced. Next add alcohol gradually, stirring all the time, until the wax floats evenly without any tendency to sink to the bottom or to rise above the surface. Then take a piece of the suspected wax, place it in the liquid and treat it in the same way. If it sinks rapidly, or rises above the surface when pushed down, it may be suspected of adulteration. If it behaves like the pure wax, it may be unsophisticated, because beeswax, from whatever country derived, has a specific gravity within very narrow limits. This test is not always to be relied upon, because the adulteration may have been accomplished with substances that are heavier or lighter in such proportions as to be nearly the same as pure wax. To determine its purity with absolute certainty the two following tests are necessary:—

A.—Place a small piece of the suspected wax in a test-tube, add some spirits of turpentine, and gently heat over a spirit lamp. If the solution is imperfect or very cloudy, or if a precipitate is formed, the wax is adulterated, for spirits of turpentine dissolves pure wax completely.

B.—A piece of wax that has successfully undergone the last test is placed in a test-tube half-filled with alcohol and boiled. Then after being allowed to cool for half an hour it is filtered. To the filtered liquid an equal amount of water is next added, also a piece of blue litmus-paper. The whole is then agitated, and if at the end of fifteen minutes the liquid remains clear, or only very slightly cloudy, and the test paper has not turned red, one may conclude that the wax is pure, if it has successfully undergone the two previous tests. On the other hand, much cloudiness and the changing to red of the test paper indicate adulteration. If wax successfully passes tests 4, A, and B, we may conclude with certainty that it is pure.

5.—To detect paraffin in wax, heat it with fuming sulphuric acid, which destroys the wax, converting it into a black jelly-like mass, while the paraffin is left as a transparent layer on the surface.

6.—The admixture of fats may be detected by the acrid odour of the vapours given off on throwing the suspected wax upon red-hot charcoal.

7.—Pure beeswax, as differing from that adulterated, may also be determined by first bumping quickly a small piece of beeswax which is known to be pure on a hot iron plate. The smell given off is noticed. Then the piece of wax to be examined is burnt in the same way. If it contains ceresin a disagreeable, fatty, white smoke is given off, which differs from the smell of wax according to the amount of ceresin mixed with it. This is a simple way of testing the purity of purchased comb-foundation.

For fuller particulars we would refer readers to Mr. Otto Hehner's paper on "The Analysis of Beeswax." in the *Analyst* of February, 1883, and to the more recent work of Messrs. A. and P. Buisine, entitled "La Cire des Abeilles (Analyse et Falsifications)." This is a most exhaustive work, and not only treats fully of analysis, but also shows how skilfully adulterations are made by mixing different substances to make the specific gravity and melting-points correspond with those of beeswax.

We will next describe the physical properties of the usual adulterants of beeswax.

VEGETABLE WAX.

All vegetables secrete more or less of a fatty substance resembling wax. This is found in different parts of a plant, either in the seeds, fruit, or on the leaves. The last are frequently covered with a thin layer of this waxy matter, which has some of the properties of beeswax. Some palms in Brazil yield a sufficient amount to make it commercially profitable to collect and send it to market.

JAPANESE WAX.—This forms an important article of export from Japan, and reaches London in large white or yellowish hard cakes, often covered with a white powdery efflorescence that adheres to the fingers. It is obtained from the fruits of *Rhus succedanea* (red lac sumach) and several other trees belonging to the *Anacardiaceæ*. The cultivation of this tree is the principal industry in the island of Kiushiu. It is also found near Nagasaki and Osaka, and the wax comes to us from those ports. The fruits are ground, and the wax, of which about 20 per cent. can be extracted, either by heating and pressure or boiling in water, is then bleached. It has a resinous and tallowy odour, melts at from 107.6 deg. to 129 deg. Fahr., and the specific gravity, unbleached, is 1.002 to 1.006, and .970 to .980 when bleached. It consists almost entirely of palmitine, is more brittle than beeswax, and breaks with a clean fracture. Japanese wax becomes translucent at about 53 deg. under its melting-point. It is sparingly soluble in cold alcohol, soluble in boiling alcohol, and on cooling forms a crystalline precipitate; hardly soluble in cold ether, but soluble in chloroform, benzol, &c. Added to beeswax, it diminishes its malleability, renders it more brittle, and lowers its melting-point. The natives use it for illumination, and in Europe it serves for adulterating beeswax. *Rhus vernicifera* (Japan lacquer-tree) also yields considerable quantities of wax.

CHINESE WAX.—This must not be confounded with Chinese insect wax, which is mentioned later. The vegetable wax is obtained from different species of *Rhus*. It is opaque-white, resembling spermaceti, harder and more brittle than Japanese wax, fibrous, easily pulverised, and crystalline. Its specific gravity is .970 and melting-point between 179.6 deg. and 181.4 deg. Fahr. It is partially soluble in alcohol or ether, but soluble in boiling naphtha, and crystallises on cooling. Used for the same purposes as Japanese wax, but raises the melting-point.

CARNAUBA WAX.—This is the product of an exudation on the surface of the leaves of *Copernicia cerifera* (Carnauba, or wax palm), which grows in abundance in Chile and Peru, and is one of the finest palms of the Brazilian forests (Fig. 34, B, Plate XVI.). The natives collect the wax in the form of a grey powder, by drying and shaking the young leaves, on the under side of which it is deposited. The powder is melted, and then the wax is cast in moulds into irregular-sized cakes of a dirty greenish-yellow or grey colour. It is hard, brittle, powders like resin, and has an aromatic odour. The refined wax has a light greenish-yellow colour and is odourless. On cooling, the melted wax cracks in all directions and has a crystalline appearance. It burns with a bright, white flame, has a specific gravity of .995 to .999, and melts between 181.4 deg. and 186.8 deg. Fahr. It is partly soluble in cold,

34, A. Ceroxylon andicola. B Copernicia cerifera. 35. "Rietsche" comb-foundation press. 36. Comb-foundation rolls.

PLATE XVII.

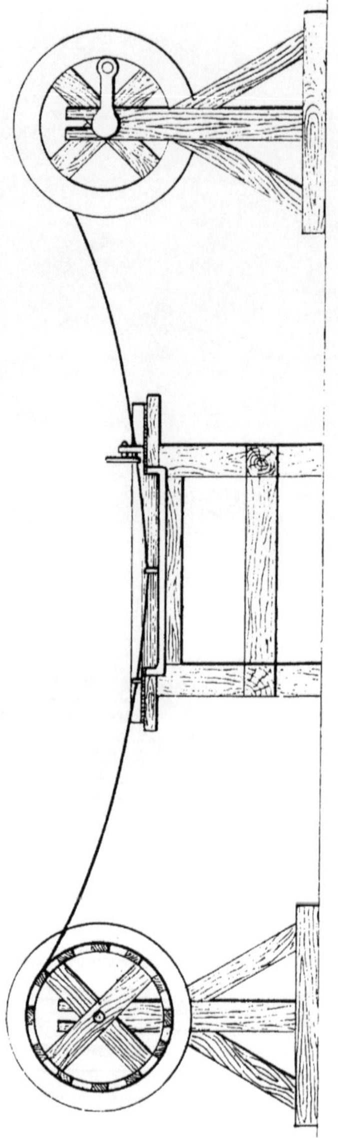

37. Apparatus for drawing wax tapers.

and soluble in boiling, alcohol, ether, and chloroform. Added to beeswax, it hardens it and raises the melting-point. Carnauba wax is a product of considerable commercial importance in Brazil, whence large quantities are sent to Europe. In 1906, 2,259,247 kilos of this wax were exported, principally from the north of Brazil. The provinces of Pernambuco, Ceara, Maranhão, and the island of Cajueiro alone exported 1,688,435 kilos, the greater part coming to England. In Brazil it is used for candle-making, and in Europe as a substitute for and an adulterant of beeswax. The increase in the exports and value of this wax, it is stated, is largely due to its use in making phonograph and gramophone records, for which it is very well suited.

SUMATRA WAX is extracted from *Ficus cerifera*, and comes from Java and Sumatra, where it is called Getah-Lahoe. The extract is a milky juice, which, after boiling, becomes a grey wax and bleaches well. It usually arrives in cakes, nearly black on the outside, pale pink inside, and is very porous. It becomes semi-fluid at 122 deg. Fahr., and melts completely at 141.8 deg. It is insoluble in cold and soluble in hot alcohol, being precipitated, on cooling, in the form of a white powder; soluble in ether, chloroform, and spirits of turpentine. Added to beeswax, it raises its melting-point.

BORNEO WAX is extracted from a species of *Sophora.* It is a good-looking, yellowish wax, with a peculiar aromatic odour. It has a crystalline texture, powdering when broken, melting at 86 deg. Fahr., and solidifying very slowly. Partially soluble in boiling alcohol, depositing, on cooling, needle-like crystals; soluble in chloroform. Lowers the melting-point of beeswax.

MYRTLE-BERRY WAX.—This is obtained from the fruit of *Myrica cerifera* and *M. caroliensis* in North America, *M. caracassana* in Colombia, and from the berries of *M. lacinata*, *M. quercifolia,* and *M. cordifolia* from the Cape of Good Hope. The berries are covered with a white wax, which melts on the berries being put into boiling water, and floats on the surface. It is a hard, greenish substance with a pleasant odour, and when purified has a pale greenish-yellow appearance. With age it becomes covered with a thin white pellicle. It is more brittle than beeswax, has a specific gravity of 1.004 to 1.015, and its melting-point is about 116.6 deg. to 120 deg. Fahr. Partly soluble in cold alcohol and ether, soluble in 4 parts of boiling ether, and 20 parts of hot alcohol. It is used in combination with beeswax for making candles, principally in the United States. The Hottentots are said to eat it like cheese.

PALM-TREE WAX is obtained from *Ceroxylon andicola* (wax palm), and comes from the Cordillera range of mountains in Colombia (Fig. 34, A, Plate XVI.). It is an exudation on the stems of the tree named, and when scraped off is obtained in small grey scales, which when melted form into a compact mass, a mixture of wax and resin, and by re-melting it is purified, and has a yellowish-white appearance; is porous and friable. Its melting-point is between 215 deg. and 221 deg. Fahr. The pure wax may be separated by digesting with boiling alcohol, when its melting-point is 161.6 deg. Fahr., and it is then similar in composition to Carnauba wax. The average yield of one tree is said to be about 25 lb. This wax forms an article of trade in Colombia, and is used by the people for making candles. A similar wax is also obtained from *Ceroxylon cerifera*, found in the Andes of Colombia and Peru.

OTOBA WAX.—This is obtained from *Myristica Otoba* (Otoba wax-tree), a native of the mountains of Colombia, *M. officinalis*, and *M. sebifera* (tallow nutmeg of Cayenne) by boiling the berries in water, when the waxy substance floats on the top. The wax is in colour a yellowish-white with a greenish tinge, and is softer than beeswax; has a specific gravity of .920, and melts at 97 deg. Fahr. The berries yield as much as 18 per cent. of wax, which is really a mixture of fatty acids and resin. It is soluble in ether and boiling alcohol, and sparingly soluble in cold alcohol. This is sometimes erroneously called Ocuba wax. Another wax similar in composition is obtained from *Myristica bicuiba*, another South American species, but its melting-point is still lower, being only 95 deg. Fahr.; it is also soluble in boiling alcohol.

COW-TREE WAX is obtained from the milky juice of *Brosimum galactodendron* (milk-tree). This so-called Cow-tree, or Palo de Leche, is regularly milked by the inhabitants of the Cordilleras of Venezuela, who, by incision, obtain an enormous quantity of a white and somewhat viscous liquid, presenting all the physical properties of the best milk, with a slight balsamic odour. It contains a large proportion of a fatty, waxy matter. When the rind of the tree is cut this milk runs out and soon thickens, assumes a grey appearance, and ceases to flow. To extract the wax the liquid is boiled and allowed to cool. The wax thus secured is of a yellowish-white colour, translucent, malleable, and melts at 140 deg. Fahr., burns well, and closely resembles beeswax.

Wax is also obtained from the seeds of *Stillingia sebifera* (Chinese wax-tree), which are covered with a very white wax, used in China for making candles. It is often mixed with insect wax.

Myrica serrata, in the Cape of Good Hope, *M. Xalapensis*, in Mexico, and *M. Faya*, from the Azores and Canaries, also produce wax, but it seldom reaches European markets.

WAX OF ANIMAL ORIGIN.

Chinese Insect Wax, or Pe La as it is sometimes called, is a secretion produced by an insect (*Coccus chinensis*), and deposited on the twigs of *Fraxinus chinensis* (Chinese ash) in the provinces of Che-Keang and Sze-Chuen, where as much as 400,000 lb. of it are gathered. It is separated from the twigs and purified, and then becomes a hard, translucent, odourless, and tasteless white crystalline body, melting at from 179.6 deg. to 186.8 deg. Fahr. In China it is largely used, mixed with tallow, for making candles. In Europe it is sometimes used for adulterating beeswax.

Spermaceti is obtained from the cachelot

whale, *Physeter macrocephalus*, and is found in the fat of this and some other species of whale. It lies principally in the head, and the mass consists almost entirely of spermaceti and oil, which is boiled, and on cooling the spermaceti congeals, and is separated by being thrown into large filter-bags, when the oil filters through, leaving the spermaceti behind. The latter is then subjected to hydraulic pressure, and melted in water, the impurities being then removed. After undergoing further refining it is poured into tin pans and allowed to cool slowly, forming a semi-transparent, brittle, lamellar, crystalline mass, tasteless and almost odourless; has a specific gravity of .950, and melts at 115 deg. to 120 deg. Fahr. It is insoluble in water, slightly soluble in cold and soluble in hot alcohol, chloroform, and carbon bisulphide. Owing to its high price it is rarely used to adulterate beeswax.

TALLOW is the concrete fat of animals, and is generally obtained from the ox and sheep. Ox tallow comes principally from Russia, while Australia sends us large quantities of mutton tallow. Its specific gravity is between .881 and .942, and it melts between 96.8 deg. and 122 deg. Fahr. It consists of variable proportions of stearine, palmitine, and oleine.

When mixed with wax this is softened and made more plastic, and it lowers its density and melting-point. It imparts a disagreeable odour and renders it greasy to the touch.

MINERAL WAX.

OZOCERIT, OZOKERIT, or CERESIN is a mineral resin found in England, the Caucasus, Transylvania, Roumania, Texas, and many other places. It is purified by means of sulphuric acid and distillation. When purified it usually goes by the name of ceresin. The colour is white with a yellow tinge, sometimes inclined to green, of a waxy consistence, and greasy in appearance; it has an aromatic odour, is flexible, and may be cut like wax, and easily kneaded when slightly warmed. The specific gravity varies from .915 to .925, and the melting-point from 140 deg. to 176 deg. Fahr., according to where it comes from. It is sparingly soluble in boiling alcohol, and is precipitated on cooling; soluble in chloroform and benzol. It is extensively used for adulterating, and as much as 20 per cent. may be added to beeswax without altering the physical properties of the latter.

The following substances are classed among

mineral waxes, and are sometimes used for adulterating beeswax:—

ZIETRISIKITE.—A mineral wax very similar to ozokerit. It is found at Zietrisika, in Moldavia, whence its name. Its behaviour is the same as that of ozokerit.

HATCHETTINE or HATCHETTITE is a waxy substance found in Glamorganshire and Moravia, near Liège, in Belgium, and a few other places. It is of greenish-yellow colour or brown, pearly in appearance, and in consistency like spermaceti. This substance is sparingly soluble in boiling alcohol and ether, leaving a viscous residue.

ELATERITE is a mineral resin, blackish in colour, verging on green, and occurs in soft, flexible masses, sometimes called mineral caoutchouc. Found near Castleton, in Derbyshire, and in the coal measures of Montrelais, in France, and melts at a very low temperature.

IDRIALINE or IDRIALITE.—A bituminous substance obtained from the mercury mines of Idria, where it occurs mixed with cinnabar. The colour is white, resembling spermaceti, and it is sparingly soluble in alcohol.

VARIOUS INDUSTRIAL PRODUCTS.

RESIN OF COLOPHONY, commonly called rosin, is obtained when common turpentine is distilled with water. That which is of brown colour is obtained from *Pinus excelsa* and the white from *Pinus maritima.* Resin is translucent, brittle, with a conchoidal fracture, pulverises readily, and is easily decomposed with heat. Its specific gravity varies between .986 and 1.108, and the melting-point is very high, being 275 deg. Fahr. It is soluble in alcohol, ether, wood alcohol, and chloroform. Added to beeswax, it makes the latter brittle and raises its melting-point considerably. It is used in connection with the adulterants previously mentioned which have a low melting-point.

STEARINE OR STEARIC ACID is obtained by the saponification of mutton tallow. After having gone through the process of manufacture it is cast into solid blocks, and on cooling affects the form of white, brilliant needles grouped together. Besides being insipid and inodorous, it has a molecular weight of .890, and melts at 158 deg. Fahr. It dissolves in all proportions in boiling anhydrous alcohol, and on cooling to 122 deg. crystallises in pearly plates. Insoluble in water, but soluble in ether, benzol, and chloroform.

Small quantities added to beeswax render it brittle and impair its malleability.

PARAFFIN is a waxy substance obtained by the dry distillation, at a low temperature, of wood, coal-tar, peat, petroleum, naphtha, and other bodies of a similar nature. The most abundant source of stearine is Boghead coal, from which it is extracted in enormous quantities. It is a white, translucent body, slightly greasy to the touch, a little softer than beeswax, and has a molecular weight of .869 to .912, while its melting-point varies between 100.4 deg. and 176 deg. Fahr., according to the source from which it is derived. It is insoluble in water, but is readily dissolved in hot olive oil, ether, oil of turpentine, benzol, chloroform, carbon bisulphide, and less readily in boiling alcohol. It is used to adulterate beeswax, which it renders translucent, dry, and brittle.

Chapter VII.

MANUFACTURE OF COMB-FOUNDATION.

IN the course of civilisation and the world's history there came a time when bees, being creatures who are wondrous builders, but know no change, failed to satisfy the needs of the modern bee-keeper so far as regards accuracy in fashioning the parallel rows of comb with which their dwellings are now furnished. The introduction of the movable frame, so necessary for easy manipulation, demanded that the combs should be built as evenly and regularly within the wooden rectangle as possible, both for convenience in handling and other purposes connected with the craft. Many devices were therefore tried with the object of attaining the desired end, such as a projecting slip of wood, a line of wax, rollers to impress the cells on a strip of wax laid on the bar, and others. These methods succeeded more or less, but they required constant time-wasting manipulations, so that all one's hopes raised were not realised, the vexation being especially great when the bee-keeper, in early spring, after putting in a frame provided with these wax impressions, found that, instead of worker-cells, superfluous drone-cells in abundance were being built.

The German carpenter J. Mehring, of Frankenthal, was the first to conceive the idea in 1857 of constructing a pair of wooden plates on which were engraved the impressions of the bases of worker-cells, and with the aid of these he impressed sheets of wax with the first foundations of comb. Schober, with Mehring's plates as a pattern, afterwards engraved the first metal plates. These were further perfected by Peter Jacob in Switzerland, Dummler in Homburg, Otto Schulz of Buckow, and others. Workable foundations were made from such plates or dies, but Mr. A. I. Root in 1875 was the first to construct a practical machine, having metal rollers embossed with indentures corresponding to the bases of the cells. Since then these machines have been much improved, so that sheets of wax now produced from those of the latest form have attained great perfection.

Two methods of producing comb-foundation are now in use, one casting and pressing in moulds, the other and more advanced form of machine impressing the wax-sheets by means of rolls.

FOUNDATION-PRESSING.—With such a presser as the "Rietsche" (shown in Fig. 35, Plate XVI.) bee-keepers are enabled to make for themselves the foundation they require. By its means the molten wax is poured on the lower plate, which has a border round it; the upper plate is then pressed down as tightly as possible, the superfluous wax being forced out at the sides. The impressed sheet of wax when removed is trimmed to size and the trimmings returned to the melting-pot. Previous to pressing, the plates are lubricated with thin starch paste or soap made into a lather, which prevents the wax from sticking to them.

Making comb-foundation with such presses, however, is wasteful, more wax being left in the sheets than is really required, seeing that, although bees readily thin down the side-walls in lengthening out the cells, they will not reduce the thickness of the midrib which forms the bases of the cells. The process is also very slow and tedious, consequently nearly all bee-keepers now use foundation made on rolls.

FOUNDATION-ROLLING. — For this purpose sheets of wax are first prepared and then passed through rollers of various designs.

Both skill and experience are, however, required in preparing the wax-sheets properly. The operation consists of dipping a thin wooden board into a deep vessel containing molten wax. A film of this adheres to the board and is afterwards peeled off. The boards are made of clean yellow pine, free from knots, and the size of sheet required. The wax must be melted in a vessel standing in an outer one containing hot water, and as this will not exceed boiling-point there is no danger of burning the wax. The dipping-tank is a vessel deep enough for holding sufficient wax when melted to allow of the dipping-boards being immersed in wax to within two inches of the upper end. Before using the boards they must be soaked in brine-water for a few hours; this soaking acts as a lubricant and prevents the grain of the wood from rising. A cooling-tank of cold water is also needed, and should stand close by.

In order to secure the best results the wax should be at a temperature of 165 deg. to 170 deg. Fahr. If too cold, ripples appear on the sheet, and if too hot, the sheets crack on being peeled off. When the sheets begin to stick to the boards the latter must be sand-papered to remove the roughness, which causes adhesion.

The number of dippings varies according to the thickness of the foundation required, from one to five dippings being needed, and the board is placed in the cooling-tank after each dipping. After each sheet has received the required number of dips and the boards are cold, the edges are scraped with a knife, one corner is pulled up, and the sheet of wax pulled off.

The sheets being now ready for rolling, the rolls are adjusted according to the thickness required and lubricated with soap lather or thin starch paste. They are then placed into a tank containing 3 in. or 4 in. in depth of salt-water, kept at a temperature of 110 deg. Fahr. At one end of this tank are placed the rolls (Fig. 36, Plate XVI.), and on the opposite side is a table for receiving the comb-foundation when finished. The temperature of the room should be kept at about 80 deg. Fahr. The sheet of wax is taken out of the tank and the end inserted between the rolls, while the crank is turned gently. As the sheet comes out on the other side it is seized with grippers and firmly held until it comes through. The sheets as they leave the rolls are laid squarely one upon another, and when the pile is 2 in. or 3 in. high a board is put on them and they are cut to the exact size required with a thin-bladed knife, dipped in starch paste to prevent it from sticking to the wax.

The greatest advance by far, however, in the production of foundation during the past few years is the invention of Mr. E. B. Weed, who in 1896 devised a method of sheeting wax which has practically superseded all others. By means of the "new process," as it is termed, a tougher and more transparent article is obtained in long sheets by passing through rollers exercising a pressure of several hundred pounds to the square inch, and when these sheets are put through the milling or embossing process the result is a foundation with the thinnest possible midrib and higher side-walls than by any former methods of production.

The new process not only produces a much superior article, but it also effects a great reduction in labour. It will be seen from the description given above that the old process involved much hand labour. By the "'Weed' New Process" this is entirely obviated, as the machines do the work automatically, one person being able to attend to them. A cake of wax is placed in the machine, and it comes out converted into a continuous sheet rolled up on a bobbin. This is then put into another automatic machine, which feeds it into the mill, and it is cut to size without any waste. The trimmed wax-sheet is then made to lie squarely on a sheet of paper, automatically pick it up, and it then settles itself on the pile, which the machine finally trues up as well as could be done by hand and very much quicker.

The A. I. Root Company are the sole makers of the "Weed" foundation machinery, but the exclusive right to manufacture "Weed" foundation in this country, along with the necessary machinery from Messrs. Root, is now the property of Messrs. James Lee and Son. It is termed "British 'Weed'" foundation, in order to distinguish it from the American product. An illustration of the "British 'Weed'" Foundation Factory is shown in Fig. 33, Plate XV.

CHAPTER VIII.

COLOURING WAX.

THERE are two methods of imparting colour to wax. One is by incorporating the pigment in molten wax, so that the whole mass becomes evenly coloured, and any article moulded from wax thus coloured shows the same tint throughout. The other plan is by applying to articles made of white wax layers of molten wax in which the various desired colours are introduced. In this case the interior is white, with an outer covering of coloured wax.

Great care should be taken not to use poisonous colours, although, as a rule, these are the brightest. They are extremely dangerous when used for making wax candles, as the heat from the flame produces noxious vapours which are highly deleterious. Candles coloured with vermilion give off mercurial vapours when alight, and those coloured with white lead produce poisonous lead fumes, and verdigris also, which is sometimes used to impart a green tint, produces dangerous vapours impregnated with arsenic acid. In addition to these, the following are most deleterious to health and should be avoided:—Cinnabar, red lead, chrome-red, chrome-yellow, and chrome-green. Finally, all colours containing mercury, copper, lead, and arsenic should be studiously avoided.

Among the harmless colours are alkanet-root, madder, and dragon's blood for red; indigo for blue; turmeric, saffron, fustic, quercitrin for yellow; indigo and turmeric for green; alkanet-root and indigo for violet; and combinations of these in different proportions will produce all colours that may be required. For instance, with a combination of alkanet-root and turmeric in varying proportions we may obtain all the different shades from light yellow to orange. A mixture of indigo and turmeric produces a green which, by increasing one or the other of these colours, gives—according to the predominance required—many different shades of green.

For coarser work the above are too costly, and the cheaper earth-colours, such as ochre, umber, burnt and raw sienna, and others, can be used to advantage.

Nothing can be found more suitable for colouring wax than aniline dyes, and by selecting those soluble in fats they readily mix with molten wax. A very small quantity is sufficient to impart the desired colour, these pigments being very penetrating; their only drawback is that when exposed to light they are liable to fade in course of time. If, however, those only soluble in water or alcohol can be obtained the wax must be kept hot until all the water or spirit has evaporated.

The wax requires melting in a pan standing in water on a couple of sticks to avoid burning, which would happen if the bottom of the vessel came in direct contact with the flame. After adding the colours, the water must be kept boiling for half an hour, when the mass is strained through canvas or linen. Suitable proportions for different tints are the following:

BLUE.—White wax, 100 parts; indigo, 6 parts.

GREEN.—White wax, 100 parts; indigo, 3 parts; turmeric, 4 parts.

YELLOW.—(1) White wax, 200 parts; powdered turmeric, 13 parts. (2) White wax, 20 parts; saffron, 1 part. (3) White wax, 100 parts; quercitrin, 9 parts.

RED.—(1) White wax, 20 parts; alkanet-root, 2 parts. (2) White wax, 100 parts; dragon's blood, 6 parts. (3) White wax, 20 parts; safflower, 2 parts.

VIOLET.—White wax, 400 parts; safflower, 12 parts; indigo, 7 parts.

BLACK.—Melt 50 parts of yellow wax and stir in 2 parts of the finest lampblack.

Chapter IX.

WAX CANDLES AND TAPERS.

ALLUSION to candles has been made in the historical chapter of this work, but it is uncertain when they were first used. Pliny mentions candles made of rushes, and we are told that in Rome the upper classes used wax and tallow candles. The very word candle is derived from the Latin *candela*, which means a light of wax. In the Middle Ages candles weighing as much as 50 lb. were made, and at that time the Britons and Anglo-Saxons used ornamental tapers in their processions.

There are several ways of making wax candles, among them the following:—(1) By dipping a wick and drawing it through melted wax; (2) by building up by hand with soft wax; (3) by pouring melted wax on wicks; (4) by pressing through a cylinder; (5) in moulds.

Candles and tapers should only be made from the best and purest beeswax, as it not only gives a better light, but is also free from the smell given off by other substances. But, as already said, owing to its high price manufacturers adulterate beeswax with numerous vegetable and mineral waxes and with tallow, the whole of which are very much cheaper and always more or less objectionable.

The most important part in the manufacture is the preparation of the wicks. These are either twisted or plaited. The former bear the appearance of a spiral, similar to the strands of a rope, the plaited wicks being made by interlacing and crossing the strands, as in ordinary straw-plaiting.

Although machinery is now extensively used in wick-making, the best are still made from cotton-rovings imported from Turkey. Four or more of these, according to the thickness of the wick, are wound off into clues and cut by machinery into such lengths as are needed for the candles in course of manufacture.

The thickness of the wicks varies proportionately to the diameter of the candles required, the number of cotton threads requisite to form the wick also varying according to their firmness. The material of which the wicks consist differs with the sort of candle required, and may be either cotton, flax, or hemp yarn. But whatever material is used, it is important that the threads are all of exactly the same thickness, free from knots, and burn slowly without leaving any residue. They are rendered less combustible by wick-mordants, composed of solutions of ammoniac salts, of bismuth, and of borates. A good mordant is a solution of $2\frac{1}{2}$ oz. boracic acid in 10 lb. of water, with $\frac{1}{3}$ oz. of strong alcohol and a few drops of sulphuric acid. If a weaker solution is used a spark will remain on the wick after the candle has been blown out, and by burning down to the wax make re-lighting difficult.

To prevent the wick from carbonising at the end, and thus obscuring the light, it is twisted with one strand shorter than the others, by means of which the wick is bent and the end pulled outside the flame, this having the effect of its being completely burnt by coming in contact with the oxygen of the air. Another way of attaining the same end is by dipping one of the wick threads in fused bismuth, and so forming a metallic wick, in which the metal fuses at the end and forms a small globule, which bends the wick over while burning. Sometimes a very fine wire is included in the wick. It must be clearly understood that all wicks must be thoroughly dried before using.

WAX TAPERS.—For these, twisted wicks only

are used, which are wound on a drum. This is placed at one end of a stand supporting a trough of melted wax, kept fluid by means of a lamp underneath it. The wick is led by means of a guide-roller into the trough, from which it passes through a series of holes in a draw-plate on to a second drum, where it is wound up (Fig. 37, Plate XVII.). To increase the thickness of the wax-coating the drums are made to change places, and the same operation is repeated. The holes in the draw-plate are progressively smaller and smaller, so that any-sized taper can be made. A little turpentine is added to the wax to render it plastic so that it may not crack as it bends over the drum. It is afterwards unrolled and cut up into lengths or wound into various-shaped rolls, some of them displaying considerable taste in the arrangement of the designs.

The short tapers used for Christmas-trees are made in the same way, the colouring on the outside being produced by drawing them through coloured wax for the last coating. These tapers, however, are now seldom made of pure beeswax, but generally have a large admixture of ozokerit. They do not burn so brightly, and give off a disagreeable smell, cheapness appearing to be their only recommendation.

Wax Candles.—These are made either by hand or with a ladle.

The large wax candles used in churches are formed by rolling the wick in a thin layer of wax, and then, after adding layer upon layer, finished off by rolling the candle by means of a long, square instrument of box, smooth at the bottom, on a table (usually made of walnut wood) until a uniform thickness of the candle is attained.

Candles are also made by hand. The wax (kept soft in hot water) is applied a small piece at a time to the wick, which latter is hung to a hook from the wall, and finished by rolling as described above, or, if the candles are small, they can be rolled between two marble slabs until a uniform thickness is attained.

Pouring Melted Wax on Wicks.—This operation is conducted in the following manner:—The wicks are first warmed in a stove and then suspended to an iron circle over a large tinned-copper basin full of melted wax. This wax is poured from a ladle over each wick in succession, the latter being sharply rotated between the fingers and thumb to prevent the wax from accumulating more on one side of the wick than on the other. When about one-third of their proper size has been reached the candles are allowed to cool for a short time, and the operation is repeated until they are half-made. This done, they are removed from the hoop and rolled, as already described. The upper end of each candle is formed by cutting it down to a metal tag which covers one end of the wick. The candles are again suspended to the hoop, but in a reversed position, and the same process of pouring on melted wax and rolling is repeated as often as necessary. The lower ends of the candles are then cut square to the desired length.

PRESSING THROUGH A CYLINDER. — Wax candles are also made by pressing soft wax through a cylinder in which the wick runs, thus forming a continuous candle, which is afterwards cut to any required length.

MOULDING.—As wax not only cools very rapidly, but also contracts while cooling, it is unsuitable for moulding. In cases, however, where moulded candles must be produced the wicks are placed in moulds made of tin and highly polished. If in one piece, they are made slightly tapering to allow of the candle being drawn out. Many moulds are made in two pieces. In the process of making, a number of such moulds are generally placed together so that they can all be filled with one pouring.

The moulds are rubbed over with an oily rag before using in order to lubricate them, otherwise the wax would stick to the metal. The wax is melted in a water-bath so that it should not become over-heated. A very good composition for moulding consists of 7 lb. of spermaceti, the latter being melted slowly over a moderate fire in a well-tinned copper kettle, and while stirring adding to it piecemeal 5 lb. of white wax.

A cheaper candle is made of 10 parts stearic acid and 1 part of white wax melted together over a water-bath. The mixture must remain in the bath for half an hour without being stirred, then the fire is extinguished, and as soon as a slight pellicle is formed on the surface it is cool enough to cast direct into the moulds, which must be previously heated to the same temperature, and allowed to cool gradually.

Fluted and spiral candles are generally made in moulds.

Chapter X.

MANUFACTURE OF WAX FLOWERS, FRUITS, AND FIGURES.

ALTHOUGH wax flowers are no longer so fashionable as in former days, a great many are still manufactured. Museums make extensive use of them for illustrating botanical specimens, some being such exquisite works of art that it is difficult to believe they are not real but only imitations in wax. None but perfectly pure beeswax is used in making, and the greatest care is taken that it contains no adulterant. None of the numerous mineral or vegetable waxes have the plasticity of pure beeswax, and they are therefore not suitable for such work.

The artist mixes a little Venice turpentine with the wax, which adds to the plasticity during the process of working, and as it evaporates in course of time, the necessary hardness is obtained. The turpentine is thoroughly boiled in water until the latter runs off quite clear, and then incorporated with the molten wax in sufficient quantity to turn the latter into a thick paste. It is then put into moulds and worked up into the desired forms. The proper proportions are 4 parts of turpentine to 50 parts of wax. To impart the required colour of natural flowers to the wax the pigments are mixed with it, as explained on page 120. In addition to this, various shadings are obtained by rubbing in dry powdered colours of the desired tints either with the fingers or various-sized stumps, with which the finest detail can be worked in.

When making wax flowers the chief materials used are sheets of wax no thicker than paper, from which are formed both petals and leaves. To make these wax-sheets strips of paper, sized and glazed, are soaked in water, and the superfluous moisture removed by placing them between blotting-paper. These damp strips are then floated on the surface of molten wax, care being taken that the wax does not flow on to the upper surface of the paper. They are then lifted off, when a thin film of wax will be found adhering, which can, by several floatings, be increased to any desired thickness. The paper is then stripped off the wax-sheets, and these are cut into the required shape with scissors or a thin, sharp knife.

Considerable experience is necessary in

preparing the wax-sheets, for if the wax be too hot, it is impossible to make a whole sheet, and if too cold, sheets of uneven thickness will result. If the wax boils and becomes frothy, the sheets will be porous. Should the paper be too wet, it is likely to tear in peeling, or if too dry, the sheet of wax will stick to it. Should the wax crack on the paper, it probably needs more turpentine, or if too soft and the sheet will not peel off easily, more wax must be added.

When flowers are made on a large scale the artist uses various-shaped cutters and polished metal moulds when forming the leaves and petals, putting them together and giving the finishing touches by hand.

When the various pieces are ready the coloured powders required are rubbed into them, copying Nature as closely as possible. Powdered asbestos is also applied if a shiny leaf is needed, and dry powdered starch put on with a camel-hair brush for producing a matt surface. In this way different colours can be made to blend in imitation of Nature. A high polish may be imparted by applying gum sandarach dissolved in alcohol with a camel-hair brush. The veining of the leaves is done by means of a stamp, or by hand with a boxwood or agate style. They are then bent into the proper shapes and securely fixed on waxed silk-covered wires of the proper thickness. The connecting parts have to be warmed in order that the wire may be embedded when pressed into the wax. The leaves prepared in this way are collected together before starting to build up the plant, the stems being first formed by covering them with plastic wax in which to hide the wires and make them appear natural. The stamens and stigmas are made of fine wire dipped in wax and coloured in the same way as the petals.

It is in his ability to imitate Nature in the final arrangement and finishing off that the skill of the artist is shown.

WAX FRUITS, FIGURES, AND MODELS.—When such large articles as figures are being made plaster-of-Paris moulds are used. These are generally constructed in two or more pieces so that when the figure is cast the mould can be easily removed. The moulds are painted over inside with shellac dissolved in spirits of wine, which fills the pores and prevents the wax from penetrating the plaster. In preparing for use the moulds are first dipped in cold water, which is allowed to run off them. Should metal moulds be used, they require lubricating with oil to prevent the wax from adhering to them. The molten wax must not be too hot, or on cooling it will shrink considerably and destroy the symmetry of the figures, while if too cool, it will not run into the finer cavities of the mould. Large figures are generally made hollow to economise wax. The moulds for these are first filled with molten wax, allowed to stand for a few minutes, and when the outside has cooled down to the desired thickness the remainder of the wax is poured out.

As beeswax is rather soft, it is usual now in making large figures to add a certain quantity of stearine or resin, or a little of both. The following are the proportions used:—

1. White wax, 4 parts; stearine, 1 part.
2. White wax, 6 parts; stearine, 1 part; resin, 1 part.
3. White wax, 12 parts; resin, 3 parts.

Very large articles may have wooden or iron braces inserted to strengthen them.

Fruit and anatomical specimens for museums are modelled in the same manner, the finishing colours being put on in the way described in making flowers.

CHAPTER XI.

TECHNICAL USES OF WAX.

PRACTICAL RECIPES.

1. MODELLING-WAX.—The wax used for this purpose is white, melted, and mixed with lard to make it malleable. In working it, the tools and the board are kept moistened with water to prevent adhesion.

2. GRAFTING-WAX.—Resin, 1 lb.; beeswax, 1 lb.; adding sufficient tallow or lard to soften so that it can be readily applied with the hand. After melting, allow it to cool, and roll the mass out on a slab into sticks.

3. SEWING-WAX.—The beeswax is usually made up into small, round cakes, about 1½ in. diameter, and gives stiffness and smoothness to sewing-thread.

4. FRENCH POLISH.—1 oz. each of gums mastic, sandarach, seed-lac, shellac, and gum arabic. Reduce to powder, then add ¼ oz. of virgin wax. Dissolve in a bottle with 1 quart of rectified spirits of wine. After standing for twelve hours it is fit for use.

5. FURNITURE PASTES.—(1) Beeswax, spirits of turpentine, and linseed-oil, equal parts. Melt and cool. (2) Beeswax, 4 oz.; turpentine, 10 oz.; alkanet-root to colour. Melt and strain. (3) *White:* White wax, 1 lb.; liquor of potassa, ½ gallon. Boil to the proper consistency. (4) Beeswax, 1 lb.; soap, ¼ lb.; pearlash, 3 oz.; dissolve in water, ½ gallon. Strain and boil, as last. (5) To keep wood light, scrape ¼ lb. of beeswax into ½ pint of turpentine.

6. FURNITURE CREAM.—(1) Beeswax, 1 lb.; soap, 4 oz.; pearlash, 2 oz.; soft water, 1 gallon. Boil together till thoroughly mixed. (2) Yellow wax, 4 oz.; yellow soap, 2 oz.; water, 50 oz. Boil, with constant stirring, and add boiled oil and oil of turpentine, each 5 oz.

7. FURNITURE OIL.—(1) Boiled linseed-oil, 1 pint; yellow wax, 4 oz. Melt, and colour with alkanet-root. (2) Alkanet-root, 1 part; shellac varnish, 4 parts; linseed-oil, 16 parts; turps, 2 parts; wax, 2 parts. Mix, and let them stand together for a week.

8. FURNITURE VARNISH.—White wax, 15 oz.; yellow resin, 1 oz. (powdered); spirits of turpentine, 1 quart. Digest until dissolved. Lay on with a brush or cloth, and well polish with a clean piece of woollen cloth.

9. FURNITURE POLISH.—(1) Beeswax, ½ lb.; alkanet-root, ¼ oz. Melt together in a pipkin until the former is well coloured; then add linseed-oil and spirits of turpentine, of each ½ gill. Strain through a piece of coarse muslin. (2) Melt 2 parts of wax, and stir into it 1 part of turpentine, after removal from the fire.

10. POLISH FOR TURNERS' WORK.—Dissolve 1 oz. of sandarach in ½ pint of spirits of wine; shave 1 oz. of bees-wax, and dissolve it in a sufficient quantity of spirits of turpentine to make it into a paste. Add the former mixture to it by degrees, then with a woollen cloth apply it to the work while it is in motion in the lathe, and polish it with a soft linen rag. It will appear as if highly varnished.

11. FLOOR POLISH.—Potash, 2 oz.; water, 2 oz. Heat to boiling-point, and gradually add, while stirring, 4 oz. of yellow wax. This done, boil up again, and pour in 9 oz. of water, and heat until a milky fluid results. This can also be used for polishing furniture.

12. VARNISH.—Boiled oil, 100 parts; finely powdered litharge, 6 parts; beeswax, 5 parts. Boil until sufficiently thick and stringy, then pour off the clear portion.

13. Table Varnish.—Oil of turpentine, 1 lb.; beeswax, 2 oz.; colophony, 1 dr. Digest the mixture for twenty-four hours; the decanted portion is then fit for immediate use.

14. White Furniture Varnish.—White wax, 6 parts; petroleum, 48 parts. Apply to the work while warm, and allow the varnish to cool; then polish by rubbing with a coarse cloth.

15. Varnish for Prints, Engravings, or Maps.—A piece of plate-glass is heated, and while yet warm a little wax is rubbed over it. Water is then poured over the plate, and the moistened picture laid thereon, and pressed closely down by means of a piece of filtering-paper. When dry, the picture is removed, and will be found to possess a surface of great brilliancy.

16. Mastic Varnish.—Gum mastic, 5 lb.; spirits of turpentine, 2 gallons. Mix with a moderate heat (carefully applied) in a close vessel, then add pale turpentine varnish, 3 pints. Mix well.

17. Common Oil Varnish.—Resin, 4 lb.; beeswax, ½ lb.; boiled oil, 1 gallon. Mix with heat, and add spirits of turpentine, 2 quarts.

18. Impermeable Varnish.—Boiled oil, 100 parts; finely powdered litharge, 6 parts; beeswax, 5 parts. Boil until sufficiently thick and stringy, then pour off the clear part.

19. Etching Varnish.—(1) White wax, 2 oz.; asphaltum, 2 oz. Melt the wax in a clean pipkin, add the asphaltum in powder, and boil to a proper consistence. Pour into warm water, and form into balls, which must be kneaded and put into taffeta for use. (2) White wax, 2 oz.; Burgundy pitch, ½ oz.; black pitch, ½ oz. Melt together, and add by degrees 2 oz. of powdered asphaltum, and boil till a drop cooled on a plate becomes brittle. (3) Soft linseed-oil, 4 oz.; gum benzoin, ½ oz.; white wax, ½ oz. Boil until only two-thirds of bulk remains.

20. Etching Varnish for Ivory.—White wax, 2 parts; tears of mastic, 2 parts. Mix well.

21. Varnish for Etching on Copper.—(1) Yellow wax, 1 oz.; mastic, 1 oz.; asphaltum, ½ oz. Melt, pour into water, and form into balls for use. (2) Tallow, 1 part; yellow wax, 2 parts. (3) Wax, 2 oz.; common turpentine, 1 dr.; olive-oil, 1 dr.

22. Varnish for Engraving on Glass.—Wax, 1 oz.; mastic, ½ oz.; asphaltum, ¼ oz.; turpentine, ½ dr.

23. Lithographic Crayon.—White wax, 4 parts; gum-lac, 2 parts. Melt over a gentle fire, then add dry tallow-soap in shavings, 2 parts. Stir until dissolved. Next add white tallow, 2 parts; copal varnish, 1 part; lampblack, 1 part. Mix well, and continue the heat and stirring until, on trial by cooling a little, it is of such hardness as to bear cutting to a fine point, and will trace delicate lines without breaking.

24. Lithographic Chalk.—Common soap, 1½ oz.; tallow, 2 oz.; virgin wax, 2½ oz.; shellac, 1 oz.; lampblack, ¼ oz. The wax and tallow are first put in an iron saucepan with a cover, and heated till the mixture will ignite. Whilst it is burning, the soap (cut into small pieces) must be thrown in, one piece at a time, taking care that the first piece is melted before adding the second. When all the soap is melted, the ingredients are allowed to continue burning till they are reduced one-third in volume. The shellac is now added, and directly the latter is melted the flame must be extinguished. The black is then added, and when completely mixed the whole is poured out on a marble slab.

25. Lithographic Ink.—(1) Tallow, 2 oz.; virgin wax, 2 oz.; shellac, 2 oz.; common soap, 2 oz.; lampblack, ½ oz. Mix as for lithographic chalk. (2) Venice turpentine, 1 part; lampblack, 2 parts; tallow, 6 parts; hard tallow-soap, 6 parts; mastic in tears, 8 parts; shellac, 12 parts; wax, 16 parts. Melt, and pour out on a slab.

26. Lithographic Transfer Ink.—Virgin wax, 2 parts; white soap, 1 part; shellac, 1 part; lampblack, ⅛ part. Mix as for lithographic chalk.

27. Autographic Ink for Lithographers.—White soap, 15 parts; white wax, 25 parts; mutton suet, 6 parts; lampblack, 6 parts; shellac, 10 parts; mastic, 10 parts. Mix with heat, and proceed as for lithographic ink.

28. Crayons for Drawing on Glass. — Melt together equal quantities of asphaltum and yellow wax, add lampblack, and pour the mixture into moulds for crayons.

29. Engravers' Border-wax.—Beeswax, 1 part; pitch, 2 parts; tallow, 1 part. Mix.

30. Black Sealing-wax.—Yellow resin, 15 lb.; lard, 1 lb.; beeswax, 1 lb.; lampblack, 3 lb. Mix with heat.

31. Soft Sealing-wax.—Yellow resin, 1 part; beeswax, 4 parts; lard, 1 part; Venice turpentine, 1 part; colour to fancy. Mix with gentle heat.

32. Gilders' Wax.—(1) Yellow wax, 3 lb.; verdigris, 1 lb.; sulphate of zinc, 1 lb.; red oxide of iron, 2½ lb. Powder the last three articles very fine. (2) Yellow wax, 7 lb.; colcothar, 7 lb.; verdigris, 3 lb.; borax, ¼ lb.; alum, ¼ lb. (3) Oil, 25 parts; yellow wax, 25 parts; acetate of copper, 13 parts; red ochre, 37 parts. The whole is melted and stirred until cold.

33. Bottle Wax.—*Black:* Black resin, 6½ lb.; beeswax, ½ lb.; finely powdered ivory black, 1½ lb. Melt together. *Red:* As the last, but substitute Venctian red, or red lead, for the ivory black.

34. Razor Paste.—Mix the finest flour-emery intimately with tallow and wax until the proper consistency is obtained in the paste, and then rub it well into the leather strop.

35. Turners' Cement.—Beeswax, 1 oz.; resin, ½ oz.; pitch, ½ oz. Melt, and stir in fine brickdust.

36. CEMENT FOR JOINING SPAR AND MARBLE ORNAMENTS.—Melt together 8 parts of resin, 1 part of wax, and stir in 4 parts, or as much as may be required, of plaster of Paris. The broken pieces to be made hot before applying the cement.

37. BOTTLE CEMENT. — Resin, 15 parts; wax, 3 parts; highly-dried red ochre, 5 parts.

38. CEMENT FOR ELECTRICAL MACHINES AND GALVANIC TROUGHS.—Melt together 5 lb. of resin and 1 lb. of beeswax, and stir in 1 lb. of red ochre (highly dried and still warm) and 4 oz. of plaster of Paris, continuing the heat a little above 212 deg. Fahr., and stirring constantly till all frothing ceases. Or (for troughs): Resin, 6 lb.; dried red ochre, 1 lb.; calcined plaster of Paris, ½ lb.; linseed-oil, ¼ lb.

39. AIR-TIGHT COVERING FOR BOTTLES, &c.—Melt india-rubber (to which 15 per cent. of wax is added) and gradually add finely powdered quick-lime till a change of odour shows that combination has taken place and a proper consistence is obtained.

40. SOFT CEMENT.—Melt yellow wax with half its weight of common turpentine and stir in a little Venetian red, previously well dried and finely powdered. This cement does very well as a temporary stopping for joints and openings in glass and other apparatus where the heat and pressure are not great.

41. MAHOGANY-COLOURED CEMENT.—Melt 2 oz. of beeswax and ½ oz. of resin together, then add ½ oz. of Indian red and a small quantity of yellow ochre to bring the cement to the desired colour. Keep it in a pipkin for use.

42. CEMENT MASTIC.—Beeswax, 2 parts; Burgundy pitch, 3 parts; resin, 8 parts. Melt and put into spring-water to solidify the paste, then roll into sticks, and in using melt only so much as is immediately required, as it becomes more brittle by repeated heating.

43. Removing Stains from Marble.—Clean with diluted hydrochloric acid or warm soap and vinegar, then heat a gallon of water, in which dissolve 1½ lb. of potash; add 1 lb. of wax, boiling the whole for half an hour, then allow to cool, when the wax will float on the surface. Put the wax into a mortar and triturate it with a marble pestle, adding soft water to it until it forms a soft paste, which, laid on marble, and when dry, rubbed with a woollen rag, gives a bright polish.

44. To Polish Alabaster.—Take white wax, melt it in a convenient vessel, and dip the cast or figure into it; withdraw, and repeat the operation of dipping until the liquid wax rests upon the surface of the cast; allow it to become cool and dry, when it may be polished with a clean brush.

45. Wax Varnish to Preserve Statues.—White wax, 2 parts; essence of turpentine, 8 parts. Melt and apply hot; spread evenly so as not to destroy the lines of the figure.

46. Waterproof Packing-paper.—Blue soap, 24 parts; white soap, 4 parts; wax, 15 parts. Boil in 120 parts of water. Dip the packing-paper into it, and after being well soaked hang up over a string to dry.

47. Waxed Paper.—Take cartridge or other paper, place it on a hot iron and rub it with beeswax, or make a solution of the wax in turpentine and apply it with a brush. Useful for making water or air proof pipes for chemical experiments, &c.

48. Waterproofing Leather.—(1) Wax, 25 oz.; Burgundy pitch, 1½ oz.; ground-nut oil, 2 oz.; iron sulphate, 1¼ oz.; essence of thyme, ½ oz. (2) India-rubber in small pieces, 1 oz.; boiled oil, 1 pint. Dissolve by heat, then add 1 pint of hot boiled oil, stir well, and cool. (3) Beeswax and yellow resin, of each 2 oz. Melt in 1 pint of boiled oil. (4) White wax and spermaceti, each 1 oz.; mutton suet, 4 oz. Melt in 1 pint of olive-oil. The above solutions should be applied while warm.

49. Waterproofing Boots and Shoes.—Beeswax, 1 oz.; suet, ½ oz.; olive-oil, 2 oz.; lampblack, ½ oz. Melt the wax and suet in the oil, add the lampblack, and stir till cool; warm the shoes and rub in the compound.

50. Wax Dubbing.—Melt together 6½ parts yellow wax, 26½ parts mutton fat, 6½ parts thick turpentine, 6½ parts olive-oil, 13 parts lard, stirring into this 5 parts of well-heated lampblack. The mass is then poured into little tin boxes for convenience in using. The dubbing is first warmed and then applied by being rubbed in well with the fingers. Hard leather is thus softened and becomes perfectly waterproof.

51. Waterproof Harness Paste.—Put into a glazed pipkin 2 oz. of black resin, place on a gentle fire till melted; add 3 oz. of beeswax, and when this also is melted remove the mixture from the fire; add ½ oz. of fine lampblack and ½ dr. of Prussian blue in fine powder. Stir till mixed well and add sufficient spirits of turpentine to form a thin paste. When cool apply a thin coat of the paste with a rag and polish with a soft polishing brush.

52. Polish for Harness.—Melt 8 oz. of beeswax in an earthen pipkin and stir in 2 oz. ivory black, 1 oz. Prussian blue ground in oil, 1 oz. oil of turpentine, and ¼ oz. copal varnish. Make into balls. Apply with a brush and polish with an old handkerchief.

53. Boot Blacking.—Ordinary starch is dissolved in hot water and wax added; the mixture is stirred and allowed to cool. Then add a small quantity of iodine to give a bluish-black colour. To 1 gallon of this mixture add 8 oz. of a solution of iron perchloride, a small quantity of gallic acid, and sometimes about 2 dr. of oil of cloves along with 8 oz. of glycerine. The whole is thoroughly stirred.

54. Nicolet's Blacking.—Dissolve 150 parts wax and 15 of tallow in a mixture of 200 of linseed oil, 20 of litharge, and 100 of molasses at a temperature of 230 deg. to 250 deg. Fahr. Then add 103 parts lampblack. When cold dilute

with 280 of spirits of turpentine. Finally mix with a solution of 5 parts of gum-lac and 2 of aniline violet in 35 of alcohol.

55. HEIN'S BLACKING.—Another shoe blacking is made by melting 90 parts beeswax, 30 of spermaceti, and 350 of spirits of turpentine with 20 of asphalt varnish, adding 10 of borax, 20 of lampblack, 10 of Prussian blue, and 5 of nitro-benzol.

56. LEATHER BLACKING.—Melt 2 lb. wax and add ¼ lb. washed and well-dried litharge by screening it through a fine sieve; then add 6 oz. ivory black and stir until cool, but not cold; add enough turpentine to reduce it to a thin paste, after which add a little birch or other essential oil to prevent it from souring.

57. HARNESS BLACKING.—Mutton suet, 2 oz.; beeswax, 6 oz.; melt them and add sugar candy, 6 oz.; soft soap, 2 oz.; lampblack, 2½ oz.; finely powdered indigo, ½ oz. When thoroughly intermixed add oil of turpentine, ¼ pint.

58. FARM HARNESS PRESERVATIVE.—Mix 1½ lb. each pure yellow wax, oil of turpentine, and castor-oil with 12½ lb. linseed-oil and 1½ lb. tar, the whole to be thoroughly mixed. By occasional application from time to time (say about every six months) harness is protected from the influence of air, heat, perspiration, and all moisture.

59. WAX SHOE POLISH.—Melt together 1 lb. of white wax, 1 lb. crown soap, 5 oz. ivory black, 1 oz. indigo, and ½ pint nut-oil. Dissolve over a slow fire, stir until cool, and turn into small moulds.

60. SHOEMAKER'S HEEL-BALL.—Beeswax, 8 oz.; tallow, 1 oz. Melt and add powdered gum arabic, 1 oz., and lampblack to colour.

61. SUPERFINE HEEL-BALL.—Melt together beeswax, 2 lb.; suet, 3 oz.; stir in ivory black, 4 oz.; lampblack, 3 oz.; powdered gum arabic, 2 oz.; powdered rock-candy, 2 oz. Mix, and when partly cold pour into tin or leaden moulds.

These balls are used not merely by shoemakers, but for copying inscriptions, raised patterns, &c., by rubbing the ball on paper laid over the article to be copied.

62. Imitation Wax Candles.—Purify melted tallow by throwing in powdered quicklime, then add 2 parts wax to 1 of tallow, and a beautiful candle closely resembling pure wax will be the result. Dip the wicks in lime-water and saltpetre on making. To 1 gallon of water add 2 oz. saltpetre and ½ lb. of lime. It improves the light and prevents the tallow from running.

63. Adamantine Candles.—Melt together 10 oz. mutton tallow; camphor, ¼ oz.; beeswax, 4 oz.; and alum, 2 oz.

64. Starch Polish.—White wax, 1 oz.; spermaceti, 2 oz. Melt together with a gentle heat. When sufficient starch is prepared in the usual way for a dozen pieces put into it a piece of the polish about the size of a large pea, more or less, according to large or small washings. This gives a beautiful gloss to linen articles.

65. Sizing for Linen.—Crystallised carbonate of soda, 1 part; white wax, 6 parts; stearine, 4 parts; pure white soap, 6 parts; fine Paris white or carbonate of magnesia, 20 parts; potato starch, 40 parts; fine wheat starch, 160 parts. Boil with sufficient water to form an aggregate of 1,600 parts, adding, if desired, sufficient ultramarine to counteract the yellow tint of the linen. The latter is saturated with this preparation and afterwards steamed and dried, then sprinkled with soap-water and placed in the stamping-mill, and lastly steamed and calendered.

66. Amalgam for Electrical Machines.—First pour into a wooden box (previously coated with chalk) 6 oz. of quicksilver; then put into a suitable iron ladle ½ oz. of beeswax, 2 oz. of purified zinc, and 1 oz. of grain tin; set the ladle over a brisk fire, and when the metals are fused pour them into the box containing the quicksilver, avoiding the dross. When cold reduce the whole to powder and mix with lard.

Keep in a box covered with tallow and spread on leather for use.

67. To Prevent Iron from Rusting.—Warm the iron till it is too hot to touch. Then rub the surface over with new and clean white wax. Return the iron to the fire and leave till it has absorbed the wax. This done, rub the surface over with a piece of serge, and the iron will not rust afterwards.

68. To Drill Hardened Steel.—Cover your steel with a coating of melted beeswax, and when cold make a circular hole in the wax with a fine-pointed needle or other article to the size required, and into it drop sufficient strong nitric acid to fill the hole thus made. An hour afterwards rinse off and apply acid again, and it will gradually eat through the metal.

69. Writing Inscriptions on Metals.—Take ½ lb. of nitric acid and 1 oz. of muriatic acid. Mix and shake well together, when it is ready for use. Warm the metal it is desired to mark till the surface will melt beeswax when the latter is applied to it. When cold the wax will have set fairly hard; then with a sharp instrument write your inscription plainly in the wax right through to the metal surface; then apply the mixed acids with a feather, carefully filling each letter. In from one to ten minutes (according to the appearance desired) the exposed surface of the metal will have been eaten away, so to speak, by the acid, and thus the inscription is engraved thereon. A free application of cold water then stops the process and the wax is removed by warming.

70. Horses' Cracked Hoofs.—Wax and honey in equal parts are melted together over a slow fire and thoroughly mixed. In using, the hoof is first thoroughly cleaned with tepid water and the above mixture then well rubbed in with a brush. After several applications the fissures and cracks disappear and the hoof regains its softness.

71. Horse Ointment.—Resin, 4 oz.; beeswax, 4 oz.; lard, 8 oz.; honey, 2 oz. Mix slowly and gently, bring to a boil, and add less than 1 pint spirits of turpentine; then remove from the fire and stir till cool. Unsurpassed for horses' cracked hoofs, &c.

USES OF WAX IN MEDICINE.

72. Remedy for Coughs, Expectoration, &c.—Breathe the vapour arising from wax when the latter is being melted on a hot iron or a brazier of charcoal.

73. Holloway's Ointment. — Butter, 22 oz.; beeswax, 3 oz.; yellow resin, 3 oz. Melt, add vinegar of cantharides, 1 oz. Evaporate, and add Canada balsam, 1 oz.; oil of mace, ½ dr.; balsam of Peru, 15 drops.

74. Corn Plaster.—(1) Beeswax, 1 lb.; resin, 4 oz.; Venice turpentine, 8 oz.; sulphate of copper, 8 oz.; arsenic, 1 oz. Mix with heat. (2) Yellow wax, 1 lb.; Burgundy pitch, 6 oz.; turpentine, 4 oz.; powdered verdigris, 2 oz. Mix with heat, and spread the composition on linen or leather, polish the surface, and cut into small pieces.

75. Tooth-stopping.—Melt 3 parts pure white wax with 3½ parts mastic, adding a few drops of oil of peppermint and making it into pills on a marble slab. The pills are pressed into hollow teeth so that food may not lodge in them and irritate the nerves.

76. Pile Ointment.—Powdered nut gall, 2 dr.; camphor, 1 dr.; melted wax, 10 oz.; tincture of opium, 2 dr. Mix and apply three times a day or as the pain may require.

77. Spermaceti Ointment.—Olive-oil, 4 lb.; white wax, 2 lb.; spermaceti, 1 lb.; water, 1½ lb. Mix and stir until cold.

K

78. SALVE FOR WOUNDS AFTER REMOVAL OF WARTS.—Prepare a salve of white wax and fresh unsalted butter in equal parts and mix a little white wine with it.

79. SALVE FOR BURNS.—A mixture of wax and linseed-oil makes an excellent plaster for burns.

80. WAX SALVE FOR SKIN DISEASES.—White wax, 5 parts; spermaceti, 5 parts; sweet almond-oil, 5 parts. Melt together in an enamelled saucepan, pour out into paper boxes, and when cold cut up into small tablets.

81. WHITE LIP-SALVE.—Olive-oil, 1 lb.; spermaceti, 1 lb.; white wax, 1 lb.; refined lard, 1 lb. Melt, and while cooling stir in rose-water, 8 oz.; essence of lemon, 2 dr.; bergamot, 2 dr.

82. RED LIP-SALVE.—Olive-oil, 1 lb.; alkanet-root, 2 oz. Macerate with heat until the oil is well coloured, then add spermaceti, 2 oz.; white wax, 8 oz.; suet (prepared), 12 oz. When nearly cold stir in orange-flower water, 1 oz.; oil of lavender, ½ dr.

83. RUSSIAN SALVE.—Take equal parts of yellow wax and sweet oil; heat and let the mixture melt slowly, carefully stirring as it does so; when cooling add a small quantity of glycerine. Good for all kinds of wounds, &c.

84. DOWNER'S SALVE.—Beeswax, 4 oz.; opium, ¼ oz.; sugar of lead, 1 oz. Melt the beeswax and work up the lead in the wax, then the opium; add 1 gill of sweet oil and incorporate the whole thoroughly together, spread lightly on cloth. Good for burns, piles, &c.

85. AMERICAN SALVE.—Burgundy pitch, beeswax, white pine pitch, and resin, 1 oz. each; mutton tallow, 8 oz.; goose oil, 1 gill; tar, 1 gill. Melt and mix thoroughly. A first-rate salve.

86. GREEN MOUNTAIN SALVE.—For rheumatism, burns, pains in the back or side, &c., use 2 lb. resin; Burgundy pitch, ¼ lb.; beeswax, ¼ lb.; mutton tallow, ¼ lb. Melt

slowly; when not too warm add oil of hemlock, 1 oz.; balsam fir, 1 oz.; oil of origanum, 1 oz.; oil of red cedar, 1 oz.; Venice turpentine, 1 oz.; oil of wormwood, 1 oz.; verdigris, ½ oz. The verdigris must be finely pulverised and mixed with the oils; then add as above, and work in cold water till the mass is cool enough to roll.

87. Green Ointment.—Honey and beeswax, each ½ lb.; spirits of turpentine, 1 oz.; wintergreen-oil and laudanum, each 2 oz.; verdigris, finely pulverised, ¼ oz.; lard, 1½ lb. Mix by a stove fire in a copper kettle, heating slowly.

88. Pills to Improve the Voice.—Beeswax, 2 dr.; copaiba balsam, 3 dr.; liquorice-root powder, 4 dr. Melt the copaiba balsam with the wax in a new earthen pipkin and make pills of 3 gr. each. Two of these pills to be taken occasionally, three or four times a day. They are the very best known for the purpose.

89. Remedy for Diarrhœa.—In France the following remedy is frequently found efficacious:—Scoop out the core of a quince, fill it with hot wax, and let it roast gently and for a long time by the fire. This is eaten before taking food for three consecutive mornings.

90. Leech Bites, to Stop.—2 parts olive oil to 1 part yellow wax, spread them on linen, and apply to the orifice.

91. Locatelli's Balsam.—Olive-oil, 1 pint; Strasburg turpentine and yellow wax, of each ½ lb.; red saunders, 6 dr. Melt the wax with part of the oil over a gentle fire, then add remaining oil and the turpentine; afterwards mix in the saunders, previously reduced to a powder, and keep them stirring together till the balsam is cold. This balsam is recommended in erosions of the intestines, dysentery, hæmorrhages, internal bruises, and in some complaints of the breast. Outwardly it is used for healing and cleansing wounds and ulcers. The dose when taken internally is from 2 sc. to 2 dr.

COSMETICAL SPECIALITIES.

92. COLD CREAM.—Oil of almonds, 5 lb.; white wax, 1 lb.; spermaceti, ½ lb. Melt by gentle heat, then stir in rose-water, 1 lb.; otto of roses, 6 drops. Used to keep the skin delicate and soft.

93. ORIENTAL COLD CREAM.—Oil of almonds, 4 oz.; white wax and spermaceti, of each 2 dr. Melt, and add rose-water, 4 oz.; orange-flower water, 1 oz. To use, apply on a cotton or linen cloth to the face, &c.

94. SHAVING CREAM.—White wax, spermaceti, almond-oil, ¼ oz. of each. Melt, and while warm beat in 2 squares of Windsor soap, previously reduced to a paste with rose-water.

95. SHAVING PASTE.—Oil of almonds, 2 parts; white soap, 2 parts; common soda, 1 part; rose-water, 1 part. Melt and perfume with otto of roses.

96. POMATUM.—Strained suet, 10 lb.; white wax, ¾ lb. Melt, then stir well in essence of bergamot, 1 oz.; essence of lemon, ½ oz.; oil of rosemary, ¼ oz.; oil of lavender, ¼ oz.; rose-water, 1 pint.

97. PLAIN, HARD POMATUM.—Lard, suet, white wax, equal parts. Mix with heat.

98. POMADE DE LA JEUNESSE.—Lard, 16 oz.; white wax, 1 oz.; dinitrate of bismuth or pearl white, 2 oz.; scent as preferred. Used as a pomade for dyeing the hair black.

99. PLAIN, SOFT POMATUM.—Olive-oil, white wax, lard, suet, equal parts. If required softer, use a little less wax or more lard and oil.

100. SOFT POMATUM.—Suet, 9 lb.; lard, 10 lb.; beeswax, 3 oz.; gum benjamin, 5 oz.; perfume to taste.

101. Pomade d'Orange.—Beeswax, 5 lb.; lard, 6 lb.; suet, 6 lb.; palm-oil, 2 lb. Melt, and while cooling stir in orange-flower water, 9 oz.; essence of neroli, 3 dr.

102. Pomade Divine.—Lard, 3 lb.; white wax, ½ lb.; balm of Gilead, 3 oz.; oil of cloves, 6 dr.; essence of bergamot, 4 dr. Melt the first two with a gentle heat, remove them from the fire, and while cooling stir in the scent.

103. Cream of Roses.—Oil of almonds, 1 lb.; rose-water, 1 pint; white wax and spermaceti, each 1 oz. Mix in a pipkin under a slight heat, then add essence of neroli, 20 drops; otto of roses, 15 drops. Put it into pots and tie over with skin or oiled leather.

104. Mille-fleurs Pomatum.—Lard and suet, each 1 lb.; white wax, 2 oz.; essence of lemon, ½ oz.; essence of musk, 90 drops; gum benzoin, 1 oz. Melt the solids, then withdraw the pot from the fire, and when partly cold stir in the essences.

105. Orange Pomatum.—Clarified lard, 7 lb.; mutton suet, 1½ lb.; yellow wax, 1½ lb.; palm-oil, ¾ lb. Melt and strain, then add, while cooling, Portugal water, ½ pint; essence of bergamot, 1 dr.; neroli, 1½ dr. Stir in well and pour into earthenware pots.

106. Soft Maréchal Pomatum.—Lard and suet, each 12 lb.; beeswax, 5 lb; maréchal powder, 12 oz. Scent. Melt the first three with a gentle heat, then add the powder and perfume.

107. Ox-marrow.—Melt 4 oz. ox-tallow; white wax, 1 oz.; fresh lard, 6 oz. When cold add 1½ oz. oil of bergamot.

108. Crême Céleste.—White wax, 1½ parts; spermaceti, 3 parts; sweet almond-oil, 3 parts. Melt together in a porcelain dish over a water bath, and when cold stir in 2 parts of rose-water.

109. GLYCERINE WAX BALSAM.—White wax, 2 parts; spermaceti, 2 parts; sweet almond-oil, 8 parts; glycerine, 4 parts; otto of roses, ⅛ part. Carefully melt together in an enamelled saucepan over a slow fire. Stir until cold and put into glass jars.

110. COSMÉTIQUE.—Melt in a porcelain dish over a water bath 500 parts of yellow wax and 125 parts of white soap; remove from the fire to cool, and before the mass has set stir in 5 parts of bergamot and 1 part of Peruvian balsam. Roll into small sticks on a glass or marble slab and cover with paper.

INDEX.

B

C

D

E

F

G

H

I

J

K

L

M

Q

R

T

U

V

W

Y

Z

http://stores.lulu.com/velvetelementbooks

www.ingramcontent.com/pod-product-compliance
Ingram Content Group UK Ltd.
Pitfield, Milton Keynes, MK11 3LW, UK
UKHW041946190726
13854UKWH00004B/1815